THE
POCKET
BOOK OF
PATRIOTS

THE
POCKET

OVER 100 BRITISH HEROES

BOOK OF

BY GEORGE COURTAULD

PATRIOTS

*'Let us now praise famous men and
our fathers that begat us'*

EBURY
PRESS

For my darling Fiona – always

First published in Great Britain in 2005

3 5 7 9 10 8 6 4 2

Text copyright © George Courtauld 2005

First published by Ebury Publishing
Random House UK Ltd, Random House, Vauxhall Bridge Road,
London SW1V 2SA

Random House Australia (Pty) Limited
20 Alfred Street, Milsons Point, Sydney, New South Wales 2061,
Australia

Random House New Zealand Limited
18 Poland Road, Glenfield, Auckland 10, New Zealand

Random House South Africa (Pty) Limited
Isle of Houghton Corner Boundary Road & Carse O'Gowrie
Houghton, 2198, P.O. Box 2002 Houghton , 2041 South Africa

Random House UK Limited Reg. No. 954009
www.randomhouse.co.uk

A CIP catalogue record for this book is available from
the British Library

Editor: Judith Hannam
Designer: Peter Ward

ISBN: 0091909015

Papers used by Ebury are natural, recyclable products made
from wood grown in sustainable forests.

Printed and bound in the UK by Mackays of Chatham Plc.

Contents

Pre-999
Boadicea 2
St Patrick 4
St Augustine 6
The Venerable Bede 8
Offa 10
Alfred the Great 12
St Dunstan 14

1000–1399
King Harold 16
William the Conqueror 18
Henry I 20
Henry II 22
Llwelyn ab Gruffydd 24
Edward I 26
Robert the Bruce 29
Edward III 31
Geoffrey Chaucer 34
Owen Glendower 36
Henry V 38

1400–99
William Caxton 41
Warwick
  the Kingmaker 43
Cardinal Wolsey 45
Sir Thomas More 47
Hugh Latimer 50
Thomas Cranmer 52
Henry VIII 54
William Tyndale 57

1500–99
Mary I 59
Elizabeth I 61
Edward VI 65
Sir Francis Drake 67
Mary Queen of Scots 69
Sir Walter Ralegh 71
Edmund Spenser 74
Christopher Marlowe 76
William Shakespeare 78
James VI/I 83
Oliver Cromwell 85

1600–99
Charles I 89
John Milton 92
George Fox 95
John Bunyan 97
Charles II 100
John Locke 103
Sir Christopher Wren 106
Sir Isaac Newton 108
Duke of Marlborough 110
William of Orange 113
Jonathan Swift 115
Sir Robert Walpole 118
Samuel Richardson 120

Contents

1700–99

John Wesley	122
Henry Fielding	126
William Pitt the Elder	129
Dr Johnson	131
Bonnie Prince Charlie	137
Adam Smith	139
Clive of India	142
Thomas Gainsborough	145
General Wolfe	147
Captain Cook	149
Edmund Burke	151
George III	154
William Blake	156
Lord Nelson	159
William Pitt the Younger	162
William Wilberforce	164
The Duke of Wellington	166
William Wordsworth	171
Jane Austen	174
J.M.W. Turner	177
John Constable	179
Elizabeth Fry	181
George Stephenson	183
Lord Palmerston	185
Lord Byron	188
Sir Robert Peel	192
John Keats	195

1800–99

Benjamin Disraeli	197
Isambard Kingdom Brunel	202
Charles Darwin	204
William Gladstone	206
William Makepeace Thackeray	209
Charles Dickens	212
Anthony Trollope	217
Queen Victoria	219
Florence Nightingale	222
Lord Kitchener	225
Cecil Rhodes	228
Edward Carson	230
Sir Edward Elgar	233
Mrs Pankhurst	235
David Lloyd George	237
Rudyard Kipling	240
Captain Scott	243
Sir Winston Churchill	245
Rupert Brooke	251
Field Marshal Slim	253

1900–99

George Orwell	255
Sir John Betjeman	258
Philip Larkin	261
Margaret Thatcher	264
Queen Elizabeth II	268

Gazetteer	271
Index	275

Introduction

IN 2004, I was lucky enough to be involved in the publication of *The Pocket Book of Patriotism* – originally a history chart I put together for my sons that evolved into a book that became a Christmas bestseller. As a headhunter spending much of my time compiling and sifting the biographies of candidates for jobs in the City, I could not resist including the potted biographies of some of our great national heroes, people I was determined my sons should know about, but who somehow did not seem to have crossed their radars at school.

People such as Boadicea and Queen Elizabeth I, Warwick the Kingmaker and the Duke of Wellington, Newton and Nelson. Sadly, in order to produce an initial print run within our budget, we had to make some cuts, including the index, the poetry and prayers and, in the end, the biographies. I was accordingly immensely gratified when Ebury Press offered to publish the missing biographies in a separate book and allowed me to add many more for good measure.

The result – this book – consists of the one hundred or so individuals who I believe did most to mould our country into what it is today. There are, of course, hundreds of others who might have been included, but these are the ones that I have chosen: My favourites, a personal choice. There are warriors, writers, churchmen and politicians. Many also are kings and queens, equally human, and yet the embodiment of an idea, a representation of power and continuity that seems to embrace and express qualities that are uniquely English, because English history is unique. The combination of our isolation as an island, our invincible navy and an industrial head-start allowed us to develop and blossom like no other nation, granting us the freedom to fashion our own laws and write our own literature, and giving us the confidence to carry them overseas, to America, India, Australia and Africa, in the name of a king or queen who symbolised not only what it was we were bringing but also what remained at home.

I was astonished when talking to journalists after the launch of *The Pocket Book of Patriotism* that so many of them were offended by the notion of patriotism, by its very existence. Perhaps they misunderstood the word. Patriotism means love of country, and we are privileged and blessed to live in a country we can love. I want my sons to love their country, to care, to know who they are and how they got here, to have that comfort, consolation and inspiration, that security and sense of belonging. I know that it will make them more complete. I know that it will make them happier.

I am not an historian, and I did not set out to make the original book all-inclusive. I wanted it to contain what I regarded as the bare essentials of our glorious National Story, to show what these heroes and heroines achieved, but also how they encouraged, enthused and inspired. How they expressed their thoughts. Their very voices. The biography format, which I use daily for my headhunting clients, is designed to give a potential employer an instant summary of a candidate's circumstances, character and career, but here I have also included quotes and it is the quotes that really bring the pages to life. These are not only some of the most magnificent words ever uttered, in a language that is perhaps our greatest contribution to humankind, but they truly allow the individuals to talk to us, like a candidate in an interview.

I have tried to make these biographies as simple as possible, without judgment, analysis or distortion. But, of course, it is not entirely accurate to claim this book contains no judgment. The judgment is in the selection, not only of the individuals themselves but of the words I have chosen to include.

So if this is my choice who am I? I am a husband, a father, a son, an Essexman and Englishman, an Anglican who was born in the mid-sixties and commutes up to London every day to pay the bills.

So often today it seems that our children are being encouraged to dwell on the drab and commonplace in history rather than the soul-stirring: the slave rather than the sovereign; the victim rather than the saviour; the helpless rather than the heroes.

What are we trying to teach them? That it is all right to be ordinary? Any father like me, who has been present at the birth of his children, knows there is no such thing as ordinary; that within minutes of being born our children each have their own looks, personalities and quirks, individual qualities and differences that make us love them from the moment we hold them in our arms.

Our forebears were extraordinary. Our children will be too.

THE
POCKET
BOOK OF
PATRIOTS

✠ Boadicea

Queen of the British tribe of the Iceni, whose kingdom was based in what is now Norfolk, she led a violent rebellion against the Romans in AD 60. Boadicea is the Latin version of her name, Boudicca, which means victory.

BIRTH	*c.* AD 20.
MARITAL STATUS	Married to Prasutagus, king of the Iceni. Two daughters.
EDUCATION	At home.
CAREER	
60	Her husband, who had co-operated with the Romans, died. Property confiscated by tax collector Catus Decianus, daughters raped and herself flogged by the Romans.
61	With the Governor and his army in Wales, Boadicea led the Iceni and Trinovantes tribes in revolt against the Romans. Raised an army of 120,000 and annihilated the ninth Roman Legion. Burnt Colchester, London and St Albans.

✠ A Little Bit of Background

The Romans re-invaded and finally conquered Britain under Emperor Claudius in AD 43. They founded London in AD 50. In AD 58, the Emperor Nero appointed a new Governor in Britain, Suetonius Paulinus, who led his army into Wales to wipe out the druids on Anglesey. By the year 60, the Romans controlled virtually all of what is now southern and central England. They had conquered Wales and the north by AD 84 and began work on Hadrian's Wall in AD 122. Britain was a peaceful, prosperous province of Rome for the next 300 years.

Some of you have been duped by the tempting promises of the Romans. Now, you have learned the difference between foreign tyranny and the free life of your ancestors. Have we not suffered every shame and humiliation? . . . I fight not for my kingdom or for booty, but for my lost freedom, my bruised body, my outraged daughters. We will win this battle or perish! That is what I, a woman, will do; men may live in slavery!

Queen Boadicea of the Iceni,
to her army, AD 60

61	Army crushed by Suetonius Paulinus in open battle near Mancetter in the West Midlands.
DEATH	AD 61, age unknown. Boadicea and her daughters escaped after the battle and committed suicide, possibly by taking poison. Reputedly buried under platform 8, King's Cross Station, London.
HOBBIES & INTERESTS	Tax avoidance.

✠ St Patrick

Saint who converted Ireland to Christianity, banished snakes, and became its Patron Saint.

BIRTH	373, in Bannavem, thought to be modern Dumbarton. He was originally called Sucat; the name Patrick comes from the Latin patrician.
MARITAL STATUS	Single.
EDUCATION	Studied under Martin of Tours, the French scholar.

CAREER

389	Captured by Picts and Scots and sold as a slave to Miliuc, a chief of Antrim, now part of Northern Ireland.
395	Made his way to Gaul, where he studied under Martin of Tours, before returning to his parents in Britain.
405	Landed in Wicklow to preach to the Irish, but met with little success. Moved to Strangford Lough, where he converted all the Ulster men. Travelled through Ireland and founded a mission settlement at Armagh.

> Today I put on
> a terrible strength
> invoking the Trinity,
> confessing the Three
> with faith in the one
> as I face my Maker.
>
> Christ beside me,
> Christ before me,
> Christ behind me,
> Christ within me,
> Christ beneath me, Christ above me.
>
> St Patrick's Breastplate

DEATH	463, aged 90. Burial spot is thought to be at the foot of Cathedral Hill, Downpatrick, Co. Down, Northern Ireland; other possibilities are Armagh and Glastonbury, Somerset. His feast day is on 17th March.
HOBBIES & INTERESTS	Nature. Used the three-leaved shamrock as a visual aid when preaching about the Trinity.

✠ *A Little Bit of Background*

Christianity arrived in Britain around AD 300. With the waning of the power of Rome, the province of Britain was raided by pirates, Picts and Scots from about AD 350. Irish monks eventually reversed Patrick's journey and brought Celtic Christianity back to England.

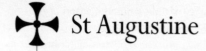

St Augustine

*The first Archbishop of Canterbury, known as the Apostle
of England, whose reintroduction of the international
Roman brand of Christianity renewed Britain's links with
the Continent.*

BIRTH	Unknown.
MARITAL STATUS	Single.
EDUCATION	By the Church.
CAREER	Prior of Pope Gregory I's Monastery of St Andrew in Rome. When Gregory saw Angle slaves he said:

'Not Angles but Angels.'

579	Sent by Gregory as a missionary to England with 40 monks. Permitted to preach by King Ethelbert (whose wife, Bertha, was already a Christian). Converted King Ethelbert. Consecrated Bishop of the English at Arles, France.

✚ *A Little Bit of Background*

The Romans abandoned Britain in the fifth century, after
which the original Romano-British Christians lost touch with Rome. The
Celtic Christianity preached by the spiritual descendants of St Patrick
was centred on monasteries and abbots rather than on bishops. By
580, however, the Saxons had consolidated their hold on the British
lowlands. The Synod of Whitby in 664, which opted for the Roman rather
than the Celtic date for Easter, confirmed the supremacy of Augustine's
Roman Church.

Founded Monastery of Christchurch, Canterbury.
Sent missionaries into Kent and Essex.

DEATH	c. 605, age unknown His feast day is 26th May.
HOBBIES & INTERESTS	The New Testament.

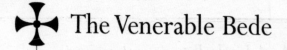 # The Venerable Bede

Monk and Saint whose History of the English Church and People, Historia Ecclesiastica Gentis Anglorum, earned him the title 'The Father of English History'. A prolific author, he wrote 40 other works.

BIRTH	*c.* 673, near Monkswearmouth, Durham.
MARITAL STATUS	Single.
EDUCATION	At Wearmouth Abbey, which boasted a library of 300–500 books.

'Such seemeth to me, my lord, the present life of men here on earth . . . as if a sparrow should come to the house and very swiftly flit through . . . which entereth in at one window and straightaway passeth out through another while you sit at dinner with your captains and servants in wintertime; the parlour being then made warm with the fire kindled in the midst thereof, but all places being troubled with raging tempests of winter rain and snow. Right for the time it be within the house it feeleth no smart of the winter storm but after a very short space of fair weather it soon passeth again from winter to winter and escapeth your sight. So the life of man here appeareth for a little season, but what followeth or what hath gone before that surely we know not. Wherefore if this new learning hath brought us any better surety, methinks it is worthy to be followed.'

Speech given by one of King Edwin of Northumbria's Saxon noblemen in favour of Christianity, *Historia Ecclesiastica Gentis Anglorum*

CAREER

680	Placed in the care of Benedict Biscop, Abbot of Wearmouth.
682	Went to Jarrow Abbey, Northumbria.
692	Ordained a deacon.

✠ *A Little Bit of Background*
The Synod of Whitby, in 664, had given the Roman Church paramountey over the Celtic Church in Britain. The Lindisfarne Gospels were illustrated around 700. Fifty years after Bede's death, the pagan Vikings began raiding in earnest.

703	Ordained a priest.
	Taught Latin, Greek and Hebrew at Jarrow Abbey.
731	Finished *Historia Ecclesiastica Gentis Anglorum*.
DEATH	735, aged 62. Originally buried at Wearmouth, his bones were moved in the 11th century to Durham Cathedral, where there is a shrine to him in the Galilee Chapel.
HOBBIES & INTERESTS	Books.

✠ Offa

King of the Angle Kingdom of Mercia 757–96 and recognised as King of the English by the Pope. Builder of Offa's Dyke, an earthwork in eastern Wales running south from the Irish Sea, near Prestatyn, to the Bristol Channel at Chepstow.

BIRTH	c. 735.
MARITAL STATUS	Married.
EDUCATION	At home.

✠ A Little Bit of Background

Between 450 and 750, Britain was settled by the Angles, Saxons and Jutes and evolved into the seven kingdoms of Northumbria, Mercia, Wessex, Essex, Sussex, Kent and East Anglia. At the very end of Offa's life, the Vikings began raiding Britain.

CAREER

757	King of the Mercians.
771	Conquered the Hestingi.
775	Defeated the Men of Kent at Otford.
	Conquered the East Saxons and took London.
779	Defeated the West Saxons at Bensington.
	Took Welsh land beyond the Severn.
	Constructed Offa's Dyke from the mouth of the Wye to the mouth of the Dee.
788	Called King of the English by Pope Hadrian I.
789	Allied with the West Saxons.
	Later allied with Northumbria.
	Codified laws later taken up by King Alfred.

789	Discovered the body of St Alban.
	Funded many monasteries.
	Made yearly payments to Rome.
	Traded with Charlemagne, King of the Franks and Holy Roman Emperor.
794	Engineered the beheading of Aethelbert, King of East Anglia.
	War with Kent and Wales.
DEATH	796, aged about 60. Where exactly he is buried is unknown. Warwickshire, Lichfield and Offlow in Staffordshire and Repton in Derbyshire are all possible sites.
HOBBIES & INTERESTS	Borders.

✠ Alfred the Great

Scholar and warrior king of Wessex, around whom a unified country evolved. The only English monarch afforded the title 'Great'.

BIRTH	849, at Wantage.
MARITAL STATUS	Married Ealhswith. Three sons, four daughters.
EDUCATION	853–6, in Rome.
CAREER	Bore the title of Secundarius, the Second, during the reign of his brother, King Ethelred I.
	Assisted his brother against the Danes.
	Fought at Aescesdun, Basing and Merton.
871	Succeeded his brother as king.
	Defeated the Danes at Wilton and agreed a treaty with them.
878	Met the second great invasion of the Danes, headed by Guthrum, which occupied Somerset.
	Defeated Guthrum at Ethandun, who agreed to be baptised and was granted the northeastern part of England, beyond Watling Street, under Alfred's overlordship.
884	War with Guthrum renewed.
	Alfred fortified London and assumed lordship over all the Saxons and Angles and several princes of Wales.
c. 890	Translated Gregory's *Liber Regulae Pastoralis* (*Pastoral Rule*).

A Little Bit of Background

The Vikings first began raiding Britain in 793. By the time Alfred reached adulthood, the Vikings were challenging the Saxons throughout Britain.

Our ancestors, who formerly held these places, loved wisdom, and through it they obtained wealth and left it to us. Here we can still see their footprints, but we cannot track after them.

Therefore it seems better to me, if it seems so to you, that we also translate certain books, which are most necessary for all men to know, into the language that we all can understand.

prose preface to *Pastoral Care*

894–7	Invasion of another great host of Vikings, in league with the Danes of East Anglia.
897	Vikings forced to withdraw, Alfred having laid the foundations of a national navy.
	Credited with dividing the country into shires and hundreds and simplifying and promoting the law.
	Attracted scholars to Wessex and, through his own writings, advanced the development of English literature.

All the Angles and Saxons, who before had been dispersed everywhere, or were in captivity with the pagans, voluntarily turned and submitted themselves to his dominion.

I gave, though in secret, boundless thanks to Almighty God, who had implanted such a love of wisdom in the king's heart.

Asser's *Life of King Alfred*, 893

DEATH	901, aged 52. Originally buried at Winchester Cathedral, his body was moved to Hyde Abbey, Winchester, in 1100.
HOBBIES & INTERESTS	Cooking.

✠ St Dunstan

The favourite of five kings, who promoted peace between the Saxons and Vikings, became Archbishop of Canterbury and, later, a saint.

BIRTH	924, near Glastonbury, son of a West Saxon noble.
MARITAL STATUS	Single.
EDUCATION	At Glastonbury Abbey.
CAREER	Became a favourite of King Athelstan, but expelled for being a wizard.
	Took monastic vows at Winchester.
	Became a favourite of King Edmund.
945	Abbot of Glastonbury; created Glastonbury School.
	Became a favourite of King Edred and also his treasurer.
952	Caused Wulfstan, the Archbishop of York and leader of the Danish faction, to be arrested.
956	Formally berated King Edwy for leaving his coronation feast to visit one of his mistresses.
	Went to Flanders.
957	Became a favourite of King Edgar.
	Made Bishop of Worcester by King Edgar.
959	Also Bishop of London.
961	As Archbishop of Canterbury, promoted the integration of the Danes.

✠ *A Little Bit of Background*

King Edgar, the first King of the English, reigned from 957 to 975, but during the reign of Aethelred the Unready the Viking invasions resumed and by 1016 Canute the Dane was King of England.

973	Crowned Edgar King of the English at Bath.

> Edgar the Glorious, by the grace of Christ illustrious King of the English.

	Dictated King Edgar's penance for 'incontinence'.
975	Crowned Edward, avoiding civil war.
	Prophesied the national disasters that would follow Edward's murder.
978	Out of favour following the murder of King Edward.
DEATH	988, aged 64. Buried at Canterbury. Relics later stolen and taken to Glastonbury, then returned to Canterbury.
HOBBIES & INTERESTS	Painting and working with metal.

King Harold

Last Saxon King of England, brave, decisive but doomed. His victory at Stamford Bridge was remarkable but his defeat at Hastings led to the end of Saxon rule in England.

BIRTH	*c.* 1019, in Wessex, second son of Godwin, Earl of East Anglia.
MARITAL STATUS	Married, 1064, Edith. Twin sons, Harold and Ulf, both of whom died in exile. Several children also by his mistress, Ealdgyth, with whom he had a 'handfast marriage'. One illegitimate daughter, Gytha of Wessex, is the ancestor to the dynasties of Galicia, Smolensk and Yaroslav. Consequently, Harold is a Russian Orthodox saint with a feast day on 14 October.
EDUCATION	In Wessex.

 ## A Little Bit of Background

Edward the Confessor was crowned in 1042, restoring the line of Wessex, but when he died, in 1066, there were at least three rival claimants to the throne. Harold's defeat by William of Normandy heralded the age of the Normans.

CAREER

1045	Earl of East Anglia.
1052	Raised forces in Ireland and sailed against the Somerset coast.
1053	Succeeded his father in Wessex.
1056	Negotiated peace between Llewellyn ab Gruffydd and the King of England.
1058	Earl of Hereford.

1059	Went on pilgrimage to Rome.
1060	His church at Waltham dedicated.
1062–3	Sailed round Wales, pillaged it, deposed Llewellyn ab Gruffydd and extorted tribute.
1064	Shipwrecked and delivered to William of Normandy, the future Conqueror. Served under him and swore on holy relics to marry his daughter and 'be his man'.
1066 Jan	Elected King by the Saxon Witan (parliament).

'I will give him seven feet of English ground, or as much more as he may be taller than other men.'

Harold's reply to the giant Harold Hardrada's request for England, *King Harald's Saga*, sect. 91, in Snorri Sturluson's *Heimskringla*, c.1260, first translated by Samuel Laing as *History of the Norse Kings*, 1844

1066 Sept	Defeated the Vikings under Harold Hardrada of Norway and Harold's own brother Tostig at the Battle of Stamford Bridge.
Oct	Defeated by the Normans at Senlac, ever since known as Battle, in the Battle of Hastings.
DEATH	1066, aged 45. Possibly buried at Waltham Abbey, though some claim that his body was hidden by the Normans to prevent his tomb becoming a shrine.
HOBBIES & INTERESTS	The sea.

William the Conqueror

King of England 1066–87 and founder of the
Norman dynasty. A ferocious ruler and immensely able
administrator, he was the last successful invader of
England.

BIRTH	1027, at Falaise, Normandy, France, the illegitimate son of Robert, Duke of Normandy, and Arlette, a tanner's daughter, and known, accordingly, as William the Bastard.
MARITAL STATUS	Married, 1053, Matilda of Flanders. Children include Robert Curthose, Alice, Cecily, William Rufus (King of England 1087–1100), Richard, Adela, Agatha, Constance, Matilda and Henry (King of England 1100–35).
EDUCATION	In Normandy.

CAREER

1035	Became Duke of Normandy.
1051	Visited England.
1052	Married Matilda of Flanders.
1054–5	Repulsed French invasion.
1058	Repulsed another French invasion.
1061	Introduced curfew, signalled by the ringing of an evening bell.
1064	Extracted oath of allegiance from Harold, Earl of Wessex (the future King Harold II of England).
1066	Invaded England and defeated Harold at Battle, 8 miles from Hastings.
	Crowned King of England at Westminster Abbey on Christmas Day.

'By the Splendour of God I have taken possession of my realm; the earth of England is in my two hands.'

Reputedly said by William after he tripped on landing at Pevensey and rose to his feet grasping sand in his hands

1067	Visited Normandy.
1068	Defeated Harold's sons at Exeter.
1069–70	Repulsed Sweyn of Denmark's invasion.
1070	Replaced Archbishop Stigand with Lanfranc.
1071	Defeated the rebel Hereward the Wake.
1072	Invaded Scotland and accepted homage from King Malcolm.
1073	Invaded Maine.
1075	Quelled Earl of Norfolk and other barons.
1078	Started work on the Tower of London
1080	Put down insurgents under his son, Robert.
1085	Commissioned the Domesday Book.
	Invaded the Vexin.

There was no single hide nor indeed was one ox, one cow or one pig not put down in his record.

If the Normans are disciplined under a just and firm rule they are men of great valour, who . . . fight resolutely to overcome all enemies. But without such rule they tear each other to pieces and destroy themselves, for they hanker after rebellion, cherish sedition, and are ready for any treachery.

Orderic Vitalis, *Ecclesiastical History*

DEATH	1087, aged 60, at Caen, France, from injuries sustained after falling from his horse.
HOBBIES & INTERESTS	Bookkeeping.

 A Little Bit of Background

Rollo the Viking became the first Duke of Normandy in 911. King Edward the Confessor of England, a Saxon, died childless in 1066. Having blackmailed Harold into swearing allegiance to him, William believed he had a valid claim to the English crown. The Normans were to rule England for the next 100 years.

King Henry I

King of England, 1100–35. His ability to read and write in a violent and illiterate age was a mark of the intelligence he applied to the affairs of state.

BIRTH	1068, traditionally at Selby, youngest and only English-born son of William the Conqueror. Nicknamed Beauclerc because he could write.
MARITAL STATUS	Married first, 1100, Matilda, daughter of Malcolm III of Scotland and Queen Margaret, who was descended from the English royal house, d. 1118. One son, William the Atheling (drowned 1120), one daughter, Matilda. Secondly, 1121, Adela of Louvain. As many as 25 illegitimate children: the largest number born to any English king.
EDUCATION	Good.

CAREER

1083	Inherited his mother's estate in England.
1088–9	Imprisoned by his elder brother, Robert Duke of Normandy.
1090	Attacked by both his brothers, Robert of Normandy and William Rufus of England.
1092	Lord of Domfront, from where he continued to fight his brother Robert.
1094	Visited England.

A Little Bit of Background

Henry I came to the throne just after the First Crusade and ruled for 35 years. Though a Norman, he married a Saxon and promoted the *Curia Regis*, the forerunner of Parliament. By his decisiveness and savagery he was able to reduce lawlessness and disorder, but in the reign of Stephen and Matilda that followed the country descended into 'The Anarchy'.

1100	On William Rufus's death, he took the treasury into his custody and was confirmed king by the Witan (the Saxon parliament). Married Matilda, daughter of Malcolm of Scotland and Queen Margaret, who was descended from the English royal house.
1101	Swapped his Norman lands with his brother Robert in exchange for the latter's claim to the English crown and a pension.
1106	Conquered the whole of Normandy anyway and forced Robert to relinquish his pension.
1107	Reformed the coinage.
1108	Captured Robert's son in Normandy.
1109	War with France.
1110	Banished barons and promoted commoners.

> An illiterate king is a crowned ass.
>
> William of Malmesbury, *De Gestis Regum Anglorum*

1114	Took his army into Wales.
1115	Forced his barons to pay homage to his heir, William, in Normandy.
1116	Forced his barons to pay homage to his heir, William, in England.
1120	Peace with France. His heir, William, lost in the wreck of the *White Ship*.
1121	Married again to Adela of Louvain. Invaded Wales and forced them to pay tribute.
1123–4	Suppressed Norman rebellion.
1131	Forced barons to swear loyalty to his daughter Matilda.
1133	Visited Normandy.
DEATH	1135, aged 67, at Angers, from overeating (a 'surfeit of lampreys'). Buried in Reading Abbey, before the High Altar.
HOBBIES & INTERESTS	Food.

King Henry II

King of England 1154–89. The first of the Plantagenets, he ruled an empire greater than that of any English king before him. He sired a line of European kings and queens, reconstructed the English legal system and focused the government on law and order.

BIRTH 1133. His mother was Matilda, daughter of Henry I.

MARITAL STATUS Married, 1152, Eleanor of Aquitaine. Four sons Henry, d. 1183, Richard (later Richard I), Geoffrey and John (later King John).

EDUCATION At Court.

A Little Bit of Background

During Henry II's reign, trial by jury became more commonplace and the Cross of St George was established as the national flag. The Pope was an Englishman, Nicolas Breakspear. Saladin, Sultan of Egypt and Syria, leader of the Muslims against the Crusaders in Palestine, captured Jerusalem.

CAREER

1151 Inherited Angevin territories.

1152 Acquired Aquitaine by marriage to Eleanor.

1154 Succeeded to English throne.

1155 Banished Flemish mercenaries and crushed rebellious barons.

1158 Retrieved border counties from Scotland and accepted tribute.

Recognised as overlord of Brittany.

Re-established the Exchequer and promoted the *Curia Regis*, forerunner of Parliament.

1159 Managed to lessen the Crown's reliance on warrior tenants.

1162	Made Thomas Becket Archbishop of Canterbury.
1166	Promoted juries in criminal matters at the Assize of Clarendon.
1166–9	Defeated Bretons.
1170	Prince Henry, his son, crowned by Archbishop of York. Accidentally provoked Becket's murder.

> 'Will no one rid me of this turbulent priest?'
>
> Of Thomas Becket, Archbishop of Canterbury, murdered in Canterbury Cathedral, December 1170

1171–2	Went to Ireland to subdue the Normans and Irish.
1173	Crushed revolt in Brittany and mutinous barons in England, thwarting the plans of his own wife and his heir, Henry.
1176–80	Established judicial circuits.
1185	Invited to deliver the Holy Land but preoccupied by a war with his sons.
DEATH	1189, at Chinon, aged 56. Buried at Fontevraud, France.
HOBBIES & INTERESTS	Architecture and war.

Llwellyn ab Gruffydd

Prince of Wales, the Last Champion of Welsh Freedom, known in Wales as Llywelyn Ein Llyw Olaf, *or Llywelyn our last leader.*

BIRTH	*c.* 1228.
MARITAL STATUS	Married, 1278, Eleanor, daughter of Simon de Montfort, who died, 1282, giving birth to their only daughter.
EDUCATION	In Wales.

CAREER

1247	Paid homage to Henry III and gave up all his lands east of the Conway.
1262	Allied to his father-in-law, Simon de Montfort, who was married to the King's youngest sister, Eleanor.
1263	Imposed truce on Prince Edward.
1265	Renewed hostilities with Henry III.
1267	Agreed to rule Wales, but subject to England.
1272	Failed to do homage to Edward I, Henry's successor.
1274	Drove Welsh competitors out of Wales.
1277	Signed Treaty of Conway.
1278	Married Eleanor de Montfort.

A Little Bit of Background

From the departure of the Romans to the arrival of the Normans, Wales was a patchwork of different tribal kingdoms. After 1066, the Norman barons moved into Wales and over the course of 200 years gradually took control of the south. Edward I, King of England from 1272 to 1307, decided to absorb Wales into his Kingdom. In 1284, the Statute of Wales brought The Principality under English control. Edward built nine massive castles to enforce his rule and created his son and heir Prince of Wales in 1301.

1282	Revolted against England.
DEATH	1282, aged 54, ambushed at Cilmeri, Wales. Head paraded round the streets of London.
HOBBIES & INTERESTS	Independence.

King Edward I

King of England 1272–1307, known as Longshanks and Hammer of the Scots. Tall, regal and articulate, he was regarded internationally as the epitome of chivalrous kingship, a law giver and warrior who advanced the unity of Britain.

BIRTH	1239, at the Palace of Westminster, eldest son of Henry III and Eleanor of Provence.
MARITAL STATUS	Married first, 1254, Eleanor of Castile, d. 1290. Sixteen children, including Edward (later Edward II). In her memory, Edward erected a series of 12 carved stone crosses, of which only three survive (at Geddington and Hardingstone in Northamptonshire, and at Waltham in Essex). The most famous of them, Charing Cross, in London, is a replica. Secondly, Marguerite of France. Three more children.
EDUCATION	At Court.
CAREER	Given Gascony, Ireland, Wales, Bristol, Stamford and Grantham by his father.
1256	Imposed the English system of counties and hundreds on Wales – provoking war.
1259	Influenced the Provisions of Oxford.
1263	War with the Welsh.
1264	Captured Simon de Montfort at Northampton. Lost the Battle of Lewes, his father, Henry III, being captured.
1265	Defeated the barons at Evesham.
1266	Subdued the Cinque Ports (Hastings, New Romney, Hythe, Dover, Sandwich and Rye). Took Kenilworth Castle.
1267	Defeated the rebel barons, who were defying him from their base on the Isle of Ely.
1268	Steward of England.

	Warden of the City and Tower of London.
1269	Abolished the levy of customs in the City.
1271	Went to Syria on a crusade.
	Relieved Acre and victorious at Haifa in the Holy Land.
1272	Stabbed with a poisoned dagger by an envoy of the Emir of Jaffa, but survived.
	Succeeded to the throne of England.
1273	Journeyed home through Europe, defeating the Count of Chalons at the 'Little Battle of Chalons', a tournament.
1274	Crowned King of England.
1275	Deliberately undermined feudalism and promoted Parliament.
	Issued the first Statute of Westminster.
1276	Subdued Llywelyn of Wales (Llwellyn ab Gruffydd).
1278	Arrested all Jews and goldsmiths in England for 'clipping coin'.
1279	Paid homage to the King of France for Ponthieu and surrendered his claim to Normandy.
1282	Conquered Wales and slew Llywelyn.
1284	Issued a Statute bringing Wales under English rule.
1285	Issued the Second Statute of Westminster.
1286–9	In France and Gascony.
1290	Expelled the Jews.
	Widowed.
	Offered to mediate in the Scottish succession and effectively appointed a Governor of Scotland.
1294	Lost Gascony.
1296	Accepted the surrender of Scotland and took the Stone of Destiny from Scone to Westminster.

A Little Bit of Background

Peterhouse, the first Cambridge college, was founded at the beginning of Edward's reign, which also saw the arrival of gunpowder in the West, the invention of the longbow and the expulsion of Jews from both England and France.

1297	Extorted a grant from the clergy for the defence of the realm. Supported the Count of Flanders against the French.
1298	Recovered Gascony. Defeated the Scottish rebel William Wallace.
1300	Reinvaded Scotland.
1301	Invested his one-year-old heir as the Prince of Wales, having promised them a prince who spoke no English!
1305	Executed William Wallace.
DEATH	1307, aged 68, at Burgh-on-Sands, on his way north to attack Robert the Bruce and reconquer Scotland. Buried in Westminster Abbey.
HOBBIES & INTERESTS	Hawking and hunting.

Robert the Bruce

Liberator of Scotland and king from 1306 to 1329. His victory at Bannockburn in 1314 forced England to accept Scotland as an independent country.

BIRTH
1274, place uncertain, possibly Turnberry Castle, Ayrshire, or Essex.

MARITAL STATUS
Married first, Isabella of Mar, through whom the crown descended to the Stuarts. One daughter, Marjorie Isabella, who died at the age of 19, soon after childbirth. Secondly, Elizabeth de Burgh. Two sons, David (later David II of Scotland) and John, and two daughters, Matilda and Margaret.

EDUCATION
Learnt Gallic, Lallans and Norman French.

CAREER

1292 Became Earl of Carrick on the death of his mother.
1296 Paid homage to King Edward I of England.
1297 Refused to go to Flanders with King Edward's army. Attacked Edward's supporters' lands in his absence.
1299 Co-regent of Scotland.

 ## A Little Bit of Background

The rival kingdoms of Scotland were never properly occupied by the Romans. They were finally united under Kenneth MacAlpin in 844, the first King of Scotland. His descendants ruled until the seven-year-old heir to the throne, Margaret, died on her journey from Norway. Thirteen rivals claimed the crown. King Edward I of England offered to mediate. He chose John Balliol, who he believed he could control. By 1296, this proved not to be the case and Edward invaded Scotland and imprisoned Balliol. William Wallace and Robert the Bruce took up the gauntlet. Wallace was executed at Smithfield in 1305, Robert was crowned in 1306.

1302–4	Professed loyalty to Edward while secretly working against him.
1306	Crowned King of Scotland at Scone.
	Defeated at Methven.
	Excommunicated and outlawed.
	Wandered in the Highlands and took refuge in a cave, where he was inspired by the determination of a spider, which failed six times to attach its web, succeeding on the seventh attempt, just as he had failed six times against the English.

> If at first you don't succeed, try try again.

1307	Victorious at London Hill.
1310	Hailed as King of Scotland by the Scottish clergy.
1312	Ceded the Hebrides by the King of Norway.
1313	Raided England.
1314	Defeated Edward II at Bannockburn.
1316	Conquered the Hebrides.
1317	Campaigning in Ireland with his brother.
1318	Took Berwick, a much disputed frontier between England and Scotland.
1320	The Declaration of Arbroath.

> It is in truth not for glory nor riches nor honours that we are fighting but for freedom – for that alone which no honest man gives up but with life itself.

1322	Thwarted Edward II's invasion and raided Yorkshire.
1323	Recognised as King of Scotland by the Pope.
1328	Made peace with Edward III.
DEATH	1329, aged 55, at Cardross Castle, on the Firth of Clyde, of leprosy. His body is buried at Dumfermline; his heart was to be buried at Jerusalem, but never got further than Melrose.
HOBBIES & INTERESTS	Freedom.

King Edward III

King of England 1327–77. Champion of the Navy, entitled by Parliament 'King of the Sea'. The greatest European warrior of his age, he put internal feuding aside to take on France and Scotland.

BIRTH 1312, at Windsor Castle, eldest son of Edward II and Queen Isabella, daughter of Philip IV of France.

MARITAL STATUS Married, 1328, Philippa of Hainault, d. 1369. Five sons, Edward (the Black Prince, father of Richard II), Lionel of Antwerp, John of Gaunt, Edmund of Langley (Duke of York) and Thomas of Woodstock (Duke of Gloucester), and five daughters.

EDUCATION At Court.

CAREER

1320	Created Earl of Chester.
1325	Received county of Ponthieu and Duchy of Aquitaine.
1326	Proclaimed guardian of the Kingdom in the name of his father.
1326–30	Puppet of his mother, Queen Isabella, and her lover, Roger Mortimer, who forfeited his claim to Scotland.

A Little Bit of Background

Edward inherited an unstable throne. His father, Edward II, had provoked the ire of the barons because of the favouritism he had shown to Piers Gaveston, with whom he was widely assumed to have had a homosexual relationship, one which ended with Gaveston's murder. During Edward III's reign, the Black Death struck. This was the most disastrous of the many outbreaks of bubonic plague, which killed one third of the British population, altering the entire structure of society.

| 1327 | King of England. |

The affairs that concern the King and the estate of his realm shall be directed by the common council of his realm and in no other wise.

1328	Married Philippa of Hainault.
1330	Executed Mortimer and imprisoned his mother the Queen.
1332	Invited Flemish weavers to England.
1333	Defeated Scots at Halidon Hill.
1337	Claimed the throne of France. The Hundred Years War begins with his invasion of France.
1339	Laid siege to Cambrai, where cannon were first used.
1340	Defeated the French Fleet at Sluys.
1344	Built the round tower of Windsor Castle.
1346	Sacked towns in France.
	Destroyed utterly the French Army at Crécy.

'Let the boy win his spurs.'

'Also say to them, that they suffer hym this day to wynne his spurres, for if god be pleased, I woll this journey be his, and the honours therof.'

Edward, speaking of his son, the Black Prince, at Crécy, 1346

1346	Defeated the Scots at Nevill's Cross, and captured the King of Scotland.
1347	Blockaded and took Calais, but spared the citizens at the request of his Queen.
1348	The Black Death strikes England.
1349	Founded the Order of the Garter.
1350	Defeated the Spanish Fleet off Winchelsea.
1351	Passed the 'Statute of Labourers and Provisors'.
1352	Passed the 'Statute of Treasons'.
1353	Passed the 'Statute of Praemunire'.
1356	Victory over the French at Poitiers. The King of France captured.
1357	Released the King of Scotland from the Tower.

1360	Withdrew all claims to the French Crown at the Treaty of Bretigny in exchange for Aquitaine, Calais, Guisnes and Ponthieu.
1362	Passed statute forcing English courts to abandon the use of the French language and instead use English.
1369	Widowed.
1374	Lost Aquitaine.
1375	The Black Prince died of the plague.

Such as thou art, so once was I. As I am now, so thou wilt be.

Inscription on the tomb of the Black Prince

DEATH	1377, of a stroke, aged 64. Buried in Westminster Abbey.
HOBBIES & INTERESTS	The sea.

Geoffrey Chaucer

English poet, spy and courtier, best known as the author of The Canterbury Tales, *often cited as the 'Father of English literature'.*

BIRTH	*c.* 1340, son of a London vintner.
MARITAL STATUS	Married, 1366, Philippa, a servant of the Duchess of Lancaster (the wife of the King's son, John of Gaunt). Three or four children.
EDUCATION	At home.

A Little Bit of Background

Edward III reigned from 1327 to 1377. The Hundred Years War between England and France began in 1337. The Black Death struck England in 1348, eventually leading to the Peasants' Revolt in 1381. John Wycliffe translated the Bible into English in 1380.

CAREER

1357	Page to the wife of the Duke of Clarence.
1359	Accompanied the Duke of Clarence to France.
	Taken prisoner in Brittany, where his writing was influenced by the French.
1360	Ransomed by Edward III.
1366	Married Philippa, a servant of John of Gaunt's wife.
1367	Awarded a pension by Edward III.
1367–9	Yeoman of the Chamber.
1369	Wrote *The Boke of the Duchess*.
	In France.
1370	Overseas 'on the King's business'.
1372	Styled himself 'Esquire'.
1372–86	Writing influenced by the Italians. Wrote *The House of Fame*, *The Parliament of Foules* and *Troilus and Criseyde*.

1372–3	In Genoa and Florence.
1374	Awarded a further pension by the King.
	Comptroller of Customs.
	Awarded pension by John of Gaunt.
1374–86	Lived in Aldgate, London.
1376–77	On secret service in Flanders.
1378	Attached to the Lombard and French embassies.
1380	Involved in the abduction of Cecilia Chaumpaigne.
1382	Comptroller of petty customs, London, with a deputy.
1385	Allowed another deputy.
1386	Knight of the Shire of Kent, relinquished both Comptrollerships.
1386–1400	Wrote *The Canterbury Tales*.

When that April with his showers soote
The drought of March hath pierced to the root
And bathed every vein in such liquor
Of which virtue engendered is the flower

The Prologue, *The Canterbury Tales*

'By God' quod he, 'for plainly at a word
thy drasty rhyming isn't worth a turd!'

The verdict of the host of the Inn at Southwark on Chaucer's work

1388	Sold his royal pensions and went on pilgrimage to Canterbury.
1389–91	Clerk of the King's Works.
1390	Robbed by highwaymen.
1391	Joint Forester of North Pemberton Park, Surrey.
1394	Awarded a pension by Richard II.
1397	Sole Forester.
1399	Awarded a further pension by Henry IV.
1400	Leased a house in Westminster.
DEATH	1400, aged *c.* 60. Buried in Westminster Abbey, where his tomb later became the focus of Poets' Corner.
HOBBIES & INTERESTS	Italian and French literature, and espionage.

Owen Glendower

Lord of Glyndwr and Sycharth, and self-styled Prince of Wales, he is known to the Welsh as Owain ab Gruffyd. A descendant of Llwellyn ab Gruffydd, he took it upon himself to rid Wales of the English, disrupting their rule for 15 years.

BIRTH	*c.* 1359, in Montgomeryshire.
MARITAL STATUS	Married Margaret Hamner. Sons included Griffith.
EDUCATION	Studied law at Westminster.

CAREER

1385	Served under Richard II in Scotland.
1386	Witness in lawsuit of Scrope *v.* Grosvenor.
	Squire to the Earl of Arundel, under Henry Bolingbroke.
1399	Rebelled against Henry when he became King Henry IV.
1400	Assumed the title Prince of Wales.
1401	Beaten back at Caernarfon.
1402	Captured Reginald de Grey and Sir Edmund Mortimer at Pilleth.
	Married Mortimer to his daughter and released him.
	Thwarted the English army.

A Little Bit of Background

Henry Bolingbroke, son of John of Gaunt, seized the throne from Richard II in 1399, becoming Henry IV. Consequently, there were always doubts about his right to the throne. The most potent challenge came from the Duke of Northumberland and his son Henry Percy (Hotspur). Owen exploited these uncertainties to win support from Northumberland and the French.

1403	His lands ravaged by Prince Henry (later Henry V).
	Took Caernarfon, Usk, Caerleon and Newport.
	Defeated, with his ally, Henry Percy (Hotspur), at Shrewsbury.
1404	Captured Harlech and Cardiff.
1405	Allied with France.
	Called a Welsh Parliament.
1406	His son captured by Prince Henry.
1407	Lost Aberystwyth.
1408	Lost South Wales.
1413	Wife and family captured.
1415	Reconciled with Henry and admitted to the 'King of England's Grace and Obedience'.
1416	Disappeared into the Welsh mountains.
DEATH	*c.* 1416, aged about 57. The exact date of his end is unknown.
HOBBIES & INTERESTS	The Law.

King Henry V

Lancastrian King of England 1413–22 and Victor of Agincourt. United his nobles and subjects in war against France, where he deployed the longbow to devastating effect.

BIRTH	1387, at Monmouth Castle. The eldest son of Henry IV, he was brought up by his uncle, Henry Beaufort.
MARITAL STATUS	Married, 1420, Catherine of France. One son, Henry (later Henry VI).
EDUCATION	Queen's College, Oxford.
CAREER	
1398–9	At the Court of Richard II.
1399	His father becomes Henry IV.
1400–3	Represented his father in Wales.
	Recovered Conway.
	Reduced Merioneth and Caernarfon.
1403	Supported his father at Shrewsbury.
1405	Relieved Coyty Castle.
1407	Took Aberystwyth and invaded Scotland.
1409	Warden of the Cinque Ports and Constable of Dover.
1413	Crowned King of England.
1414	Suppressed the Lollards, the followers of the heretic John Wycliffe.
1415	Demanded French, Norman and Angevin territories.

A Little Bit of Background

Between 1378 and 1415 there were rival popes at Avignon and Rome. In 1420, the Portuguese, under Prince Henry the Navigator, began exploring West Africa.

1415 | Took Harfleur and challenged the Dauphin to single combat. Commanded the centre at the Battle of Agincourt on 25th October, the Feast of Crispian.

This day is call'd the feast of Crispian:
He that outlives this day, and comes safe home,
Will stand a tip-toe when this day is nam'd,
And rouse him at the name of Crispian.
He that shall live this day, and see old age,
Will yearly on the vigil feast his neighbours,
And say, 'Tomorrow is Saint Crispian':
Then will he strip his sleeve and show his scars,
And say, 'These wounds I had on Crispian's day'.
Old men forget: yet all shall be forgot,
But he'll remember with advantages
What feats he did that day. Then shall our names,
Familiar in his mouth as household words,
Harry the king, Bedford and Exeter,
Warwick and Talbot, Salisbury and Gloucester,
Be in their flowing cups freshly remember'd.
This story shall the good man teach his son;
And Crispin Crispian shall ne'er go by,
From this day to the ending of the world,
But we in it shall be remembered;
We few, we happy few, we band of brothers;
For he to-day that sheds his blood with me
Shall be my brother; be he ne'er so vile
This day shall gentle his condition:
And gentlemen in England now a-bed
Shall think themselves accurs'd they were not here,
And hold their manhoods cheap whiles any speaks
That fought with us upon Saint Crispin's day.

Henry V, Act IV, sc. III, William Shakespeare

Victory over much larger French force.
Granted Custom on Wool and Tonnage and Poundage by Parliament for life.

1416 | Involved in healing the Papal schism.

1417	Personally led the successful assault on Caen.
1417	Conquered Normandy.
1420	Signed the Treaty of Troyes, in which he was accepted as heir to the French Crown and Lord of Normandy.
	Married Catherine of France.
	Defeated the Sire de Barbazan in single combat.
	Reformed Benedictine monasteries.
	Took his wife to England to be crowned.
1421	Relieved Chartres and drove the Dauphin across the Loire.
1422	Took Meaux.
DEATH	1422, aged 35, from fever, at Bois de Vincennes, on his way to help Burgundy. He is buried in Westminster Abbey.
HOBBIES & INTERESTS	Jousting.

William Caxton

The first English printer, who was also a great translator and businessman.

BIRTH	*c.* 1421, at Tenterden, in Kent.
MARITAL STATUS	Married.
EDUCATION	Apprentice cloth dealer.

 ## A Little Bit of Background

Caxton lived his life in the context of the Wars of the Roses. The Lancastrian Henry VI reigned from 1422 to 1461, having inherited the throne from his father, Henry V, before his first birthday. He was deposed by the Yorkist Edward IV, although he was briefly restored to the throne by Warwick the Kingmaker in 1471. The German Gutenberg first used movable type in 1454 to produce his Bible. In 1489, plus and minus symbols began to be used in mathematics.

CAREER

1438	Apprenticed to a London mercer (a cloth-dealer).
1441	Went to Bruges, Belgium.
1446–70	Merchant in Bruges.
1465–9	Governor of British Merchants in the Low Countries.
1469–71	In Bruges, translating *Recuyell of the Historyes of Troye*.
1471–6	In Cologne, Germany, where he learned the art of printing.
1474	Printed *Le Recueil des Histoires de Troye* at his own press in Bruges.
1475	Printed *The Game and Playe of the Chesse*, which he had also translated from French.
1476	Returned to England.
1477–91	Set up his press at Westminster, where he produced nearly 80 books, including Malory's *Le Morte D'Arthur*.

The worshipful father and first founder and embellisher of ornate eloquence in our English, I mean Master Geoffrey Chaucer.

epilogue to Caxton's edition of Chaucer's translation of Boethius' *De Consolatione Philosophiae*, c. 1478

It is notoriously known through the universal world that there be nine worthy and the best that ever were. That is to wit three paynims, three Jews, and three Christian men. As for the paynims they were . . . the first Hector of Troy . . . the second Alexander the Great; and the third Julius Caesar . . . As for the three Jews . . . the first was Duke Joshua . . . the second David, King of Jerusalem, and the third Judas Maccabaeus . . . And sith the said Incarnation . . . was first the noble Arthur . . . the second was Charlemagne or Charles the Great . . . and the third and last was Godfrey of Bouillon.

prologue to *Le Morte D'Arthur*, Thomas Malory, 1485

I, according to my copy, have done set it in imprint, to the intent that noble men may see and learn the noble acts of chivalry, the gentle and virtuous deeds that some knights used in those days.

prologue to *Le Morte D'Arthur*, Thomas Malory, 1485

DEATH	1491, aged 70.
HOBBIES & INTERESTS	Chess.

Warwick the Kingmaker

Richard Neville, Earl of Warwick and Salisbury. Powerful baron who, for 20 years, manipulated the succession and influenced the crown of England.

BIRTH | 1428, at Bisham, Berks, eldest son of Richard, Earl of Salisbury.

MARITAL STATUS | Married, as a boy, Anne de Beauchamp, daughter of the Earl of Warwick, whose title and estates he inherited. Two daughters, Isabel and Anne Neville.

EDUCATION | In England.

CAREER

1449 | Succeeded to his father-in-law's titles and estates.

1453 | Backed Richard, Duke of York, protector of England, during the Lancastrian Henry VI's insanity.

1455 | Supported Richard at the first Battle of St Albans.

1456 | Awarded the Captaincy of Calais.

1457 | Negotiated with Philip of Burgundy.

1458 | Participated in the 'Love-day' Procession.
Attacked Spanish fleet off Calais.

1459 | Captured five massive, armed Spanish merchant ships.

1459 | At Ludlow with the Duke of York.
Dismissed from Captaincy of Calais by Henry's wife, Queen Margaret. Refused to comply.

 ## A Little Bit of Background

The Hundred Years War between England and France ended in 1453. Two years later The Wars of the Roses broke out, fought between rival Yorkist and Lancastrian claimants to the English throne. The conflict began in 1455, with the Battle of St Albans, and did not end until the Battle of Bosworth 30 years later.

1460	Welcomed by London. Victory at Northampton. Took Henry VI to London.
	The Duke of York's and Warwick's own fathers killed.
1461	Became Earl of Salisbury, KG, and Great Chamberlain.
	Lost control of King Henry to Queen Margaret at the second Battle of St Albans.
1461	Declared Edward, the new Duke of York, King.
	Defeated Lancastrians at Towton.
	Duke of York crowned King Edward IV. Guided by Warwick for first three years.
1464	Disapproved of the King's marriage to Elizabeth Woodville and her family's influence.
1467	Left Court.
1469	Married his daughter to the Duke of Clarence.
	Encouraged the revolt of Robin of Redesdale.
1470	Temporarily imprisoned Edward.
	Defeated by Edward at Stamford. Escaped to France.
	Joined the Lancastrians. Returned to England.
	Proclaimed Henry VI King. Edward fled to Flanders.
1471	Fought Edward at the Battle of Barnet.
DEATH	1471, aged 43, at the Battle of Barnet. Buried at Bisham Abbey.
HOBBIES & INTERESTS	The Crown of England.

Cardinal Wolsey

English cardinal, courtier and Lord Chancellor during the
reign of Henry VIII. For 15 years one of the most powerful
men in England, until he failed in his promise to engineer
the King's divorce from Catherine of Aragon.

BIRTH	*c.* 1475, son of an Ipswich butcher, Robert Wulcy.
MARITAL STATUS	Single.
EDUCATION	Magdalen College, Oxford.

 ## A Little Bit of Background

Protestant reformer Martin Luther published his *95 Theses* in 1517. Henry VIII reigned from 1509 to 1547.

CAREER

1497	Fellow of Magdalen College, Oxford.
	Master of School attached to Magdalen.
1498–9	Junior Bursar, Magdalen College.
1499–1500	Senior Bursar, Magdalen College.
1500	Rector of Limington.
1501	Chaplain to the Archbishop of Canterbury.
1503	Chaplain to Sir Richard Nanfan.
1507	Chaplain to King Henry VII.
1509	Dean of Lincoln and then Prebendary of Lincoln Cathedral.
	Almoner to the new king, Henry VIII.
1510	Bachelor of Divinity and Doctor of Divinity, Oxford.
	Prebendary of Hereford Cathedral.
1511	Canon of Windsor, Registrar of the Order of the Garter and a Privy Councillor.
1512	Dean of Hereford.

1513	Dean of York, then Dean of St Stephen's Westminster and Precentor of London.
1514	Bishop of Lincoln.
	Archbishop of York.
1515	Cardinal and Lord Chancellor.
1518	Granted administration of the Bishopric of Bath and Wells.
1520	Accompanied Henry VIII to the Field of the Cloth of Gold, a series of meetings near Calais between Henry VIII and Francis I of France.
1522	Negotiated Treaties for Henry and the Pope.
1524	Resigned Bishopric of Bath and Wells and accepted that of Durham. Turned the monastery of Saint Frideswide into Christ Church College, Oxford.
1527	Supported Henry VIII's divorce.
1529	Resigned Bishopric of Durham and accepted that of Winchester.
	Bill of Indictment preferred against him in the King's Bench, as a result of the delays over arranging Papal sanction of Henry's divorce from Catherine of Aragon and marriage to Anne Boleyn.
1530	Received Royal Pardon.
	Arrested for high treason.

'Father Abbot, I am come to lay my bones amongst you.'

Negotiations of Thomas Wolsey, George Cavendish, 1641.

Had I but served God as diligently as I have served the King, he would not have given me over in my grey hairs.

Negotiations of Thomas Wolsey, George Cavendish, 1641.

DEATH	1530, aged 55, at Leicester, on his way to London and almost certain execution.
HOBBIES & INTERESTS	Education.

Sir Thomas More

*English lawyer, scholar and saint who, as Henry VIII's
Lord Chancellor, 1529–32, dared to oppose the King's
assumption of the leadership of the English Church. As the
creator of the imaginary island of* Utopia, *he added a new
word to the English language.*

BIRTH | 1478, Cripplegate, London, the son of a judge.

MARITAL STATUS | Married first, Jane Colt, d. 1411. Four children.
Secondly, Alice Middleton.

EDUCATION | St Anthony's School, Threadneedle Street, London.
The Household of Archbishop of Canterbury.
Canterbury Hall, Oxford.

 ## A Little Bit of Background

Henry VIII assumed the Governorship of the English Church,
the opposition to which cost More his life, in order to divorce Catherine of
Aragon and marry Anne Boleyn. Once free from the control of the Pope,
Henry dissolved the monasteries and set England on a Protestant course.

CAREER

1494	Entered at New Inn to study law.
1496	Joined Lincoln's Inn, and called to the Bar.
1504	Elected a Member of Parliament.
1508	Visited Paris and Louvain.
1509	Bencher at Lincoln's Inn.
1510	Under-Sheriff of London.
1511	Reader of Lincoln's Inn.
1515	Envoy to Flanders to negotiate Treaty. Whilst he was away, he dreamed up an imaginary island called Utopia.
1516	Published *Utopia*.
1516	Member of Embassy to Calais.

1518	Master of Requests and Privy Councillor (having impressed Henry VIII defending the Pope's interests in the Star Chamber).
1520	Present at the Field of the Cloth of Gold, a series of meetings near Calais between Henry VIII and Francis I of France.
1521	Knighted.
	Under-Treasurer of England.
	Went to Calais and Bruges with Cardinal Wolsey.
1522	Given land in Oxfordshire.
1524–32	High Steward of Oxford University.
1525	Given land in Kent.
	High Steward of Cambridge University.
	Chancellor of the Duchy of Lancaster.
1527	Negotiating at Amiens.
1528	Published his *Dialogue*, a rebuttal of the views of Protestant reformist William Tyndale.
1529	Negotiating at Cambrai.
1529–32	Lord Chancellor.
1534	Imprisoned in the Tower for refusing to approve the King's divorce or admit any reduction in the Pope's authority.
	Wrote *Dialogue of Comfort against Tribulation*.

'By god body, master More, *Indignatio principis mors est* [The anger of the sovereign is death].'

'Is that all, my Lord?' quoth he (to the Duke of Norfolk). Then in good faith is there no more difference between your grace and me, but that I shall die today, and you tomorrow.'

Life of Sir Thomas More, William Roper, 1626

'We may not look at our pleasure to go to heaven in feather-beds; it is not the way.'   *Life of Sir Thomas More*, Ibid.

1535	Indicted for High Treason.

'I pray you, master Lieutenant, see me safe up, and my coming down let me shift for my self.'   *Life of Sir Thomas More*, William Roper

'Pluck up thy spirits, man, and be not afraid to do thine office; my neck is very short; take heed therefore thou strike not awry, for saving of thine honesty.'

Thomas More's words to the executioner, ibid.

'This hath not offended the King!'

On clearing his beard from the block, ibid.

DEATH	1535, aged 57, beheaded. His head was displayed on London Bridge for a month. His daughter bribed the man supposed to throw it in the Thames and is thought to have had it buried in the Roper Vault at Canterbury Cathedral. His body is buried in the Church of St Peter ad Vincula, at the Tower.
HOBBIES & INTERESTS	The Law.

Hugh Latimer

Bishop of Worcester and Protestant martyr who became the embodiment of English resistance to religious persecution.

BIRTH — c. 1485, Thurcaston, Leicestershire, son of a yeoman.

MARITAL STATUS — Single.

EDUCATION — Christ's College, Cambridge.
Fellow of Clare College, Cambridge.

CAREER

1525	Refused to deny the doctrines of Luther.
	Forced to explain himself before Cardinal Wolsey.
1529	Preached 'sermons on the card'.
1530	Master in Theology, Oxford.
	Preached to Henry VIII at Windsor.
1532	Accused of heresy, but absolved when made a complete submission.
1535	Bishop of Worcester.
1537	Gave sermon at Jane Seymour's funeral.
1539	Resigned in protest at the Act of the Six Articles.
	Imprisoned for a year.
1548	After eight years' silence, preached the 'Sermon of the Plough'.

A Little Bit of Background

Henry VIII came to the throne in 1509. The Protestant reformer Martin Luther published his *95 Theses* in 1517. William Tyndale published his English translation of The New Testament in 1526. Henry's Protestant son, Edward VI, was crowned in 1547, but was succeeded in 1553 by his Catholic sister, Bloody Mary, whose reign was marked by the persecution of Protestants.

> *Gutta cavat lapidem, non vi sed saepe cadendo.*
> The drop of rain maketh a hole in the stone, not by violence, but by oft falling.
>
> The Second Sermon preached before the King's Majesty, 19 April 1549

1553	Committed to the Tower by Bloody Mary.
1554	Defended his views before theologians at Oxford.
1555	Condemned as a heretic.

> 'Be of good comfort, Master Ridley, and play the man; we shall this day light such a candle, by God's grace, in England as I trust shall never be put out.'
>
> Words spoken to Nicholas Ridley as they were about to be burnt, 1555

DEATH	1555, aged 70. Burnt at the stake in Oxford with fellow heretic Nicholas Ridley.
HOBBIES & INTERESTS	Theology.

Thomas Cranmer

Archbishop of Canterbury and creator of the Book of Common Prayer. *His act of defiance on being burned at the stake was an inspiration to Anglicans.*

BIRTH	1489, Nottingham.
MARITAL STATUS	Married. He sacrificed his fellowship of Jesus College, Cambridge, to do so.
EDUCATION	Philosophy, logic and classics at Jesus College, Cambridge.

A Little Bit of Background

When Henry VIII died in 1547, he was succeeded for six years by his son, Edward VI. When Henry's Catholic daughter, Bloody Mary, came to the throne, she initiated a five-year campaign to return England to the Catholic Church.

CAREER	
1529	Speculated out of the pulpit that Henry VIII could divorce Catherine of Aragon.
	Then repeated the suggestion in a treatise.
1530–33	Aide of the English Ambassador to Charles V of Spain.
1533	Appointed Archbishop of Canterbury and formally condemned Henry VIII's marriage to Catherine of Aragon, pronouncing it invalid.
	Affirmed legality of the King's marriage to Anne Boleyn and his position as supreme Lord of the Church of England.
1536	Condemned Henry's marriage to Anne Boleyn, pronouncing it invalid.
1547	Appointed to the council that would govern until Edward VI became of age.
1548	In charge of producing the first prayer book.
1552	Revised by him and authorised in the Act of Uniformity.

Issued 42 articles of religion, eventually reduced to the *39 Articles*.

Give us grace, that, being not like children carried away with every blast of vain doctrine, we may be established in the truth of thy holy gospel.

St Mark's Day, Collect, *Book of Common Prayer*

Almighty God, unto whom all hearts be open, all desires known, and from whom no secrets are hid; Cleanse the thoughts of our heart by the inspiration of thy holy spirit, that we may perfectly love thee and worthily magnify thy holy name.

Holy Communion, Collect, *Book of Common Prayer*

With this ring I thee wed, with my body I thee worship and with all my worldly goods I thee endow.   Marriage Service, *Book of Common Prayer*

1553	Imprisoned in the Tower by Queen Mary for backing Lady Jane Grey and attacking the Mass.
1554	Freed to explain his heresy in Oxford. Formally condemned.
1555	Charged to appear before the Pope.
1556	Refused to recognise Papal authority.
	Dismissed as Archbishop.
	Signed documents admitting the truth of Roman Catholic doctrine (except for transubstantiation – the belief that the bread and wine in the sacrament are converted to the body and blood of Christ) and the leadership of the Pope.
DEATH	1556, aged 66. Burned at the stake in Oxford. Just before being burned, he was due to make his recantation public, but he instead used the occasion to retract.

'This was the hand that wrote it, therefore it shall suffer first punishment.'

On plunging his right hand into the flames.

HOBBIES & INTERESTS	The Church of England.

King Henry VIII

King of England 1509–47. Savage, greedy and imperious, his break with Rome, precipitated by Catherine of Aragon's failure to provide him with a male heir, destroyed the old medieval culture, initiating a social, economic and religious revolution.

BIRTH

1491, Palace of Placentia, Greenwich, second son of Henry VII.

MARITAL STATUS

Married six times: *i* Catherine of Aragon, 1509, marr. diss. 1533, one daughter, Mary; *ii* Anne Boleyn, 1533, executed 1536, one daughter, Elizabeth; *iii* Jane Seymour, 1536, d. 1537, one son, Edward; *iv* Anne of Cleves, 1540 marr. diss. 1540; *v* Catherine Howard, 1540, executed 1542; *vi* Catherine Parr, 1543.

EDUCATION

At Court.

CAREER

1494 Lieutenant of Ireland.

1502 Became Prince of Wales on the death of his elder brother, Arthur.

1503 Engaged to Catherine of Aragon, the daughter of the King of Spain, his brother's 17-year-old widow.

1509 King of England.

1510 Executed his father's henchmen, Empson and Dudley.

1511 Backed his father-in-law against the Moors.
In league with the Pope against France.

1513 Won the 'Battle of Spurs' against the French. The Scots being defeated in his absence at Flodden.

1514 Made peace with France.

1515 Made Cardinal Wolsey Chancellor.

1520 Competed with the King of France on the Field of the Cloth of Gold, a series of meetings near Calais between Henry and Francis I.

1521	Wrote *Assertio Septem Sacramentorum*, attacking the views of the Protestant reformer Martin Luther, and was made Defender of the Faith by the Pope.
1527	Began negotiating with the Pope to divorce Catherine.
1529	Dismissed Cardinal Wolsey for failing to arrange Papal sanction of his divorce from Catherine and marriage to Anne Boleyn.
1530	Consulted Italian, French and English universities, helped by Thomas Cranmer, about his divorce, and acquired, through bribery, eight favourable judgements.
1531	Acknowledged by English clergy as Supreme Head of the English Church. Separated from Catherine. Married Anne Boleyn in secret.
1533	Anne publicly crowned. Appointed Cranmer Archbishop of Canterbury. Excommunicated by the Pope.
1534	Abolished Roman revenues and jurisdiction in England. Imprisoned Thomas More and John Fisher, Bishop of Rochester, and executed the Nun of Kent and her followers.
1535	Executed More and Fisher for refusing to accept him as Head of the Church.
1536	Beheaded Anne Boleyn. Married Jane Seymour. Took Wales into political union with England.
1536–7	Crushed risings in the East and North (The Pilgrimage of Grace).
1538	Death of Jane Seymour, shortly after giving birth to a male heir.

A Little Bit of Background

Machiavelli wrote *The Prince*, a treatise on statecraft, in 1516. The Diet of Worms, in 1521, marked the start of the Reformation. In 1529, the Ottoman Turks were at the gates of Vienna. The Jesuits were founded in 1534. The French Protestant reformer Calvin was in Geneva in 1546.

1539	Dissolved monasteries, but abandoned talks with German Protestants and maintained Catholic doctrine.
1540	Executed remaining Yorkists. Married Anne of Cleves.

> The King found her so different from her picture . . . that . . . he swore they had brought him a Flanders mare.
>
> Of Anne of Cleves, *A Complete History of England*, Tobias Smollett, vol. 6, 3rd ed., 1759

1540	Divorced Anne of Cleves. Executed Thomas Cromwell, reputedly for providing him with such a hideous wife. Married Catherine Howard. Burned several Protestants for heresy.
1542	Beheaded Catherine Howard. Claimed his feudal right to Scotland and defeated James V.
1543	Married Catherine Parr.
1544	Burned Leith and Edinburgh.
1545	Took Boulogne.
1546	Made peace with France.
1547	Beheaded the Earl of Surrey. Completed Cardinal Wolsey's College at Oxford (Christ Church) but changed the name to Henry VIII's College.
DEATH	1547, aged 55, at the Palace of Whitehall, from an infected wound. He is buried at St George's Chapel, Windsor.
HOBBIES & INTERESTS	Jousting and music (he composed numerous ballads, many of which are now lost, including *Pastyme with Good Companie*, though not, as is commonly thought, *Greensleeves*).

William Tyndale

English translator of the Bible and Protestant martyr.

BIRTH	*c.* 1494, possibly at Slymbridge, Gloucestershire.
MARITAL STATUS	Married.
EDUCATION	Magdalen College, Oxford, and then Cambridge.

 ## A Little Bit of Background

At the time that Tyndale's translation was beginning to circulate, Henry VIII was deciding on divorce. When Tyndale was executed at Antwerp, Calvin was in Geneva.

CAREER

1516–22	Preached in Gloucestershire. Translated Erasmus's *Enchiridion Militis Christiani*, a manual of simple piety according to the teachings of Jesus.
1523	In London. Declared his intention to translate the New Testament into English.

'If God spare my life, ere many years I will cause a boy that driveth the plough shall know more of the scripture than thou doest!'

1524	Completed translation in Hamburg and visited Protestant reformer Martin Luther at Wittenberg.
1525	Began printing his translation at Worms, but obstructed by the Senate at Cologne.
	Finished printing at Worms and introduced copies into England.
1526	Translation denounced by the Bishops. Copies seized and destroyed.

1526	Escaped to Marburg, under the protection of Philip the Magnanimous, Landgrave of Hesse.
	Became a follower of the Swiss Protestant reformer Huldreich Zwingli.
1528	Published *Parable of the Wicked Mammon* and *The Obedience of a Christian Man*.
1529	Went to Hamburg and Antwerp.
1530	Wrote *The Practyse of Prelates* denouncing Bishops, Wolsey and Henry VIII's divorce proceedings.
	Translated the Pentateuch.
1531	Wrote *An Answere unto Sir Thomas Mores dialoge* and translated The Book of Jonah.
	On learning of Henry VIII's orders to have him kidnapped, fled Antwerp.
1533	Returned to Antwerp and arrested by Imperial Officers for heresy.
1535	Imprisoned at Vilvorde.

> 'Lord, open the King of England's eyes!'
>
> His last words, 1536

DEATH	1536, at Vilvorde Prison, Antwerp, where he was strangled and then burnt at the stake.
HOBBIES & INTERESTS	Printing.

Queen Mary I

Queen of England and Ireland 1553–8, and wife of Philip of Spain, whose brutal attempt to return England to the Roman Catholic Church achieved the opposite effect and earned her the soubriquet 'Bloody Mary'.

BIRTH	1516, only surviving child of Henry VIII and Catherine of Aragon.
MARITAL STATUS	Married, 1554, Philip of Spain.
EDUCATION	Studied Greek, Latin, French, Italian, science and music.

 ## A Little Bit of Background

When it was obvious that Edward VI's illness would lead to his death, he nominated a fellow Protestant, Lady Jane Grey, as his heir. She was Queen for nine days in July 1553. Having rallied the people to her standard, Mary then squandered their good will by her savage persecution of Protestants, executing 300. Her marriage to Philip of Spain and then the loss of Calais, last vestige of a once proud empire, condemned her in the eyes of her subjects.

CAREER	
1525	Made Princess of Wales at Ludlow Castle.
1532	Separated from her mother.
1533	Declared illegitimate.
	Proclaimed Queen.
	Released Catholics held in the Tower.
	Announced intention to reintroduce Catholicism and marry Philip, heir to the Spanish throne.
1554	Executed Lady Jane Grey.
	Married Philip.
	Expelled married clergy and attacked Protestantism.
	Imagined herself pregnant.

1555	Executed 96 Protestants.
	Argued with Philip, who returned to Spain.
1558	Lost Calais.

> When I am dead and opened, you shall find
> 'Calais' lying in my heart.
>
> *Holinshed's Chronicles*, vol. 4, 1577

DEATH | 1558, aged 42. Buried in Westminster Abbey.

HOBBIES & INTERESTS | Music.

Queen Elizabeth I

Queen of England and Ireland, 1558–1603. Arguably England's greatest monarch, she inherited a throne torn between Puritanism and Roman Catholicism. She promoted the Protestant Church, defeated the Spanish Armada and presided over an unrivalled national rebirth.

BIRTH	1533, at Greenwich Palace, only child of Henry VIII and Anne Boleyn.
MARITAL STATUS	Single.
EDUCATION	By governesses, 'Muggie' and 'Kat'. Learnt Latin and Greek.
CAREER	
1536	Declared illegitimate.
1553	Rode by her half-sister Queen Mary's side, on Mary's triumphant entry into London.
1554	Imprisoned in the Tower.
1558	Proclaimed Queen.

'This is the Lord's doing and it is marvellous in our eyes.'

On hearing of her accession

 A Little Bit of Background

After the agony of Bloody Mary's reign, Elizabeth refrained from persecuting Catholics but embraced Protestantism as a patriotic necessity. Protestants were massacred in France on St Bartholomew's Day in 1572. The Battle of Lepanto, in 1571, ended the Turkish threat to Europe from the sea. Sir Walter Ralegh established the American colony of Virginia in the Queen's honour in 1584. The Edict of Nantes granted tolerance to French Protestants in 1598.

1559	Crowned.
	Played three suitors off against each other.
1560	Insisted the French quit Scotland.

'The queen of Scots is this day leichter of a fair son, and I am but a barren stock.'

To her ladies, June 1566, quoted in *Memoirs of His Own Life*, Sir James Melville, 1827 edition

'I am your anointed Queen. I will never be by violence constrained to do anything. I thank God that I am endued with such qualities that if I were turned out of the Realm in my petticoat, I were able to live in any place in Christome.'

Speech to members of Parliament, 5 November 1566, quoted in
Elizabeth I and her Parliaments, 1559–1581, J.E. Neale, 1953, pt 3, ch.1

1568	Imprisoned her cousin, Mary, Queen of Scots.
1570	Excommunicated by the Pope.

'I would not open windows into men's souls.'

Oral tradition, quoted in *Reign of Elizabeth 1558–1603*, J.B. Black, 1936

1572	Executed the Duke of Norfolk, a Catholic, for treason.

'My Lord, We have forgot the fart.'

To Edward de Vere, Earl of Oxford, 1572, on his return from seven years of self-imposed exile, occasioned by the acute embarrassment to himself of breaking wind in the presence of the Queen, quoted in *Brief Lives*, 'Edward de Vere', John Aubrey

1573	Declined Sovereignty of the Low Countries.

'Twas God the word that spake it,
He took the bread and brake it;
And what the word did make it;
That I believe, and take it.

Answer on being asked her opinion of Christ's presence in the Sacrament, quoted in
The Marrow of Ecclesiastical History, pt 2, bk 1, 'The Life of Queen Elizabeth', S. Clarke, 1675

1586	Executed conspirators in the Babington Plot, an incompetent

conspiracy to assassinate the Queen and put Mary Queen of Scots on the throne.

'I know what it is to be a subject, what to be a Sovereign, what to have good neighbours, and sometimes meet evil-willers.'

Speech to a Parliamentary deputation at Richmond, 12 November 1586, quoted in *Elizabeth I and her Parliaments 1584–1601*, from a report 'which the Queen herself heavily amended in her own hand', Sir John Neale, 1957

'I will make you shorter by the head.'

To the leaders of her Council, who were opposing her course of action towards Mary Queen of Scots, quoted in *Sayings of Queen Elizabeth*, F. Chamberlain, 1923

1587 Signed Mary Queen of Scots' Death Warrant.
1588 Reviewed troops at Tilbury and defeated Spanish Armada.

'I know I have the body of a weak and feeble woman, but I have the heart and stomach of a king, and of a king of England too; and think foul scorn that Parma or Spain, or any prince of Europe, should dare to invade the borders of my realm.'

Speech to the troops at Tilbury on the approach of the Armada, 1588, quoted in *A Third Collection of Scarce and Valuable Tracts*, Lord Somers, 1751

'My lord, we make use of you, not for your bad legs, but for your good head.'

To William Cecil, who suffered from gout, 1590, quoted in *Sayings of Queen Elizabeth*, F. Chamberlain, 1923

1599 Made her favourite, the Earl of Essex, Governor General of Ireland. He promptly lost the Queen's favour by making an unauthorised treaty and returning to England without permission.
1601 Revoked monopolies.
Executed Essex for rebellion.

'Though God hath raised me high, yet this I count the glory of my crown: that I have reigned with your loves.'

The Golden Speech, 1601, quoted in *The Journals of All the Parliaments*, collected by Sir Simonds D'Ewes, 1682

'God may pardon you, but I never can.'

To the dying Countess of Nottingham, February 1603, for her part in the death of the Earl of Essex; the story is almost certainly apocryphal. Quoted in *The History of England under the House of Tudor*, David Hume, 1759, vol. 2, ch. 7

'Must! Is must a word to be addressed to princes? Little man, little man! Thy father, if he had been alive, durst not have used that word.'

To Robert Cecil, on his saying she must go to bed, shortly before her death

'All my possessions for a moment of time.'

Last words

DEATH	1603, aged 69, at Richmond. Buried in Westminster Abbey.
HOBBIES & INTERESTS	Dresses.

King Edward VI

Boy King of England between 1547 and 1553, he was the only male heir of Henry VIII. Though initally guided by his Protestant uncle, he is justly regarded as the Champion of the English Reformation.

BIRTH 1537, Palace of Placentia, Greenwich, son of Henry VIII and Jane Seymour.

MARITAL STATUS Single.

EDUCATION Learnt Greek, Latin, French, music and astronomy.

A Little Bit of Background

Henry VIII broke with Rome but remained wary of Protestantism. Edward had no such doubts and was wholly committed to making England fully Protestant.

CAREER

1547 Crowned King of England
Knighted by his uncle, the Earl of Hertford, Protector of England.
Made Hertford the Duke of Somerset.
Made John Knox and the Bishops Ridley and Latimer Court preachers.

1549 The first *Book of Common Prayer* published.

Man that is born of woman hath but a short time to live, and is full of misery.　　　Burial of the Dead, *Book of Common Prayer*, 1549

We have left undone those things which we ought to have done; and we have done those things we ought not to have done.
　　　Morning Prayer, General Confession, *Book of Common Prayer*, 1549

> Defend, oh Lord, this thy child with thy heavenly grace that he may continue thine forever; and daily increase in thy holy spirit more and more, until he come unto thy everlasting kingdom.
>
> Order of Confirmation, *Book of Common Prayer*, 1549

1551	Betrothed to Princess Elizabeth of France.
1552	Agreed to the execution of the Duke of Somerset.
1553	Ravaged by consumption.
	Donated the Palace of Bridewell to the Corporation of London as a workhouse.
	Converted Grey Friars Monastery into Christ's Hospital, a school for the education of poor London children.
DEATH	1553, aged 15, of tuberculosis, or possibly arsenic poisoning, administered as a cure, at Greenwich.
HOBBIES & INTERESTS	Astronomy and playing the lute.

Sir Francis Drake

English sailor and explorer who exemplified the dash and gallantry of Elizabethan England.

BIRTH	*c.* 1540, Plymouth.
MARITAL STATUS	Married first, 1569, Mary Newman, d. 1583. Secondly, Elizabeth Sydenham.
EDUCATION	At sea.

 ## A Little Bit of Background

Throughout Elizabeth's reign, from 1558 to 1603, Catholic Spain threatened the very existence of Protestant England.

CAREER

1567	Commanded the *Judith*, one of six ships in John Hawkins' unsuccessful piratical expedition against the Spanish.
1570–2	Three voyages to the West Indies.
1572	Burnt and plundered Portobello, Panama.
1573	Sacked Venta Cruz.
1575	Served in Ireland and reduced Rathlin.
1577	Sailed from Plymouth for the River Plate, South America.

'I must have the gentlemen to haul and draw with the mariner, and the mariner with the gentleman . . . I would know him, that would refuse to set his hand to a rope, but I know there is not any such here.'

Drake and the Tudor Navy, J.S. Corbett, vol. 1, ch. 9, 1898

1578	Sailed through the Strait of Magellan.
1579	Plundered Valparaíso, Chile.
1580	Rounded the Cape of Good Hope.

1581	Knighted by Elizabeth at Deptford.
1582	Mayor of Plymouth.
1583	Survived assassination attempts by agents of Spain.
1584–5	MP for Bossiney.
1585	Given command of a fleet of Queen's Ships and Letters of Marque by Queen Elizabeth.
1586	Took San Domingo and Cartagena, Colombia.
	Brought first colonists of Virginia back home.
1587	Commissioned to commit acts of war against Spain.
	Destroyed armaments at Cadiz.

There must be a beginning of any great matter, but the continuing unto the end until it be thoroughly finished yields the true glory.

Dispatch to Francis Walsingham, Secretary of State to Elizabeth, 17 May 1587

'I have singed the King of Spain's Beard.'

On the expedition to Cadiz, 1587

1588	Defeated the Spanish Armada off Gravelines and chased it to the North of Scotland.

'There is plenty of time to win this game, and thrash the Spaniards too.'

Reputed reply after being told of the sighting of the Armada during a game of bowls

1590	Improved the water supply of Plymouth.
1593	MP for Plymouth.
1595	Commanded expedition to the West Indies.
DEATH	1596, aged 56, off Portobello, Panama.
HOBBIES & INTERESTS	Bowls.

Mary Queen of Scots

Queen of Scotland 1542–67, the great hope of Catholic Europe as the potential saviour of Catholic England and the mother of James I.

BIRTH

1542, at Linlithgow, only daughter of James V of Scotland and Mary of Guise, and great-granddaughter of Henry VII of England.

MARITAL STATUS

Married three times: *i* Francis II of France, 1558, d. 1560; *ii* Earl of Darnley, 1565, murdered 1567, one son, James VI/I *iii* Earl of Bothwell, 1567, diss. 1570.

EDUCATION

At the French Court, with the royal children of France, but not taught English.

CAREER

1542 Became Queen of Scotland on the death of her father when only six days old.

1558 Married Francis, the French Dauphin, signing a secret treaty delivering Scotland to France should she die without issue.

Claimed the English Crown on the death of Mary I.

1559–60 Queen of France.

1560 Widowed at the age of 17.

1561 Returned to Scotland.

1562 Fell out with Protestant reformer John Knox, who accused her of idolatry.

1563 Her favourite, Chastelard, who had accompanied her from France, was found hidden in her bedroom and executed.

1565 Married the Earl of Darnley.

1566 Marched on Glasgow to capture mutinous nobles.

Quarrelled with Darnley, who was then implicated in the brutal murder of her secretary, Riccio.

Gave birth to James, the future VI of Scotland and I of England.

1567	Invited Darnley to accompany her to Edinburgh, where, with her probable connivance, the house he was staying in was blown up, killing him.
	Three months later married the Earl of Bothwell.
	Imprisoned in Lochleven and offered a choice between divorce, trial (for Darnley's murder) or abdication in favour of her one-year-old son. She chose abdication.
1568	Escaped, lost the Battle of Langside and fled to England.
	Imprisoned in Carlisle and then Tutbury and then Wingfield.
1569	Accepted Norfolk's proposal of marriage (though still married to Bothwell) and joined plot for Catholic rising.
1570	Marriage to Bothwell dissolved by the Pope.
	Suggested conquest of England to Pope and Philip of Spain.
1584	Bequeathed her crown to Philip.
1586	Imprisoned in Tutbury and Chartley.
	Involved in the Babington Plot, a conspiracy to assassinate Elizabeth I.

'Look to your consciences and remember that the theatre of the world is wider than the realm of England.'

To the commissioners appointed to try her at Fotheringhay, 13 October 1586, quoted in *Mary Queen of Scots*, Antonia Fraser, 1969, ch. 25

Tried at Fotheringhay Castle and condemned.

En ma fin git mon commencement [In my end is my beginning].

Motto embroidered with an emblem of her mother, Mary of Guise, and quoted in a letter from William Drummond of Hawthornden to Ben Jonson, 1619

| **DEATH** | 1587, aged 44, beheaded at Fotheringhay Castle. |
| **HOBBIES & INTERESTS** | Writing poetry. |

Sir Walter Ralegh

English explorer, courtier and poet, credited with
introducing tobacco and potatoes to England. He was also
a generous patron, and brought Edmund Spenser to Court.

BIRTH	*c.* 1552, at Hayes Barton, Devon.
MARITAL STATUS	Married, 1593, Elizabeth Throgmorton, a maid of honour at Court. Two sons, Walter and Carew.
EDUCATION	Oriel College, Oxford.

 ## A Little Bit of Background

Elizabeth I, who reigned from 1558–1603, had an eye for dashing young men. Ralegh benefited from her interest but had less allure for her successor, King James.

CAREER

1569	Served in France in the Huguenot Army.
1578	Went on a 'voyage of discovery' with his half-brother, Sir Humphrey Gilbert.
1580	Captain of company in Ireland.
1581	Sent to England with dispatches, where he caught the eye of the Queen and remained at Court.

Our passions are most like to floods and streams;
The shallow murmur, but the deep are dumb.

'Sir Walter Ralegh to the Queen'

Fain I would climb, yet fear I to fall.
(The Queen replied, 'If thy heart fails thee, climb not at all.')

Written on a windowpane, quoted in *History of The Worthies of England*, 'Devonshire', Thomas Fuller, 1662

1584	Knighted.
	Obtained a patent to take possession of unknown lands in America in the Queen's name.
1585	Land christened Virginia.
1586	Land abandoned.
1588	On a commission to draw up a plan to defend England from a Spanish Invasion

> A maze wherein affection finds no end,
> A ranging cloud that runs before the wind,
> A substance like the shadow of the sun,
> A goal of grief from which the wisest run.
>
> 'Farewell False Love', Sir Walter Ralegh, 1588

1588	Quarrelled with the Queen's new favourite, the Earl of Essex.
1592	Imprisoned in the Tower, the Queen having discovered his 'association' with Elizabeth Throgmorton.
	Released.
1593	Marrried Elizabeth Throgmorton anyway, and was forbidden from Court.
	Settled in Sherborne, Dorset.
1595	Expedition to South America in search of the City of Gold.
1596	Expedition against Cadiz.
1597	Expedition against the Azores.
1603	Accused of conspiring against James I and imprisoned in the Tower.

> Give me my scallop-shell of quiet,
> My staff of faith to walk upon,
> My script of joy, immortal diet,
> My bottle of salvation,
> My gown of glory, hope's true gage,
> And thus I'll take my pilgrimage.
>
> 'The Passionate Man's Pilgrimage', Sir Walter Ralegh, 1604

1614	Published the first volume of his *History of the World*, which reached no further than the 2nd century BC.

Say to the court, it glows
And shines like rotten wood;
Say to the church, it shows
What's good, and doth no good:
If church and court reply,
Then give them both the lie.

'The Lie', Sir Walter Ralegh, 1608

1616	Released from the Tower to explore the Orinoco in search of gold.
1618	Returned to England, having failed to find gold but burnt a Spanish settlement His arrest demanded by the Spanish.

Even such is Time, which takes on trust
Our youth, our joys, and all we have,
And pays us but with age and dust;
Who in the dark and silent grave,
When we have wandered all our ways,
Shuts up the story of our days:
And from which earth, and grave, and dust,
The Lord shall raise me up, I trust.

Written the night before his death and found in his Bible in the Gate-House at Westminster

''Tis a sharp remedy, but a sure one for all ills.'

On feeling the edge of the axe, quoted in *History of Great Britain* , vol. 1, ch. 4, D. Hume, 1754

'So the heart be right, it is no matter which way the head lies.'

At his execution, on being asked which way he preferred to lay his head, quoted in
Sir Walter Raleigh, ch. 30, W. Stebbing, 1891

DEATH	1618, aged 66, executed in Old Palace Yard, Westminster. Buried in St Margaret's, Westminster.
HOBBIES & INTERESTS	Poetry.

Edmund Spenser

Author of the epic poem The Faerie Queene, *the title of which suggested both the idea of glory and its embodiment in Elizabeth I. The stanza form he invented (eight lines of ten syllables followed by one of 12 syllables) was later used by Keats and Shelley.*

BIRTH	c. 1552, in East Smithfield, London, son of a joinery man and clothmaker.
MARITAL STATUS	Married, 1594, Elizabeth Boyle. One son, Peregrine.
EDUCATION	Merchant Taylors' School; Pembroke College, Cambridge.

 ## A Little Bit of Background

Elizabeth was proclaimed Queen in 1558 and was still on the throne when Spenser died. *The Faerie Queene* alludes to a number of contemporary events, such as the execution of Mary Queen of Scots in 1587, the defeat of the Spanish Armada in 1588 and the development of the Anglican Church.

CAREER

1578	Obtained a place in the household of the Earl of Leicester.
1579	Published *The Shepheardes Calendar* and began *The Faerie Queene*.

> And he that strives to touch the stars
> Oft stumbles at a straw.
>
> *The Shepheardes Calendar,* 'July', l. 99

1580	Appointed Secretary to the Lord Deputy of Ireland. Went to live in Ireland.
1586	Published 'Astrophel', an elegy on Sir Philip Sidney.

1588	Acquired a castle and estate near Cork.
1589	Published the first instalment (three books) of *The Faerie Queene.*
1590	Published *Complaints*, containing 'sundrie small poems of the world's vanitie'.
1594	Married Elizabeth Boyle.
1595	Published *Colin Clouts come home again.*
	Celebrated his marriage in *Epithalamion.*
1596	Published the remaining three books of *The Faerie Queene* and *Foure Hymnes.*

> Sleep after toil, port after stormy seas,
> Ease after war, death after life does greatly please.
>
> *The Faerie Queene,* Bk I , Canto 9, st. 40

1598	Fled to Cork, his castle having been burnt by locals.
1599	Returned to England.
DEATH	1599, aged 47, in poverty, in King Street, Westminster. Buried in Westminster Abbey.
HOBBIES & INTERESTS	Elizabeth I.

Christopher Marlowe

Playwright and spy, author of Tamburlaine the Great, Doctor Faustus *and* The Jew of Malta, *he had a profound influence on English writing, including that of his contemporary, William Shakespeare.*

BIRTH	1564, Canterbury, son of a cobbler.
MARITAL STATUS	Single.
EDUCATION	King's School, Canterbury; Corpus Christi, Cambridge, where he is thought to have written *Dido, Queene of Carthage* (published 1594).

 ## A Little Bit of Background

While Marlowe was writing *The Jew of Malta*, the Spanish Armada was bearing down on England. With Protestants and Catholics at loggerheads all over Europe, his atheism and blasphemy were deemed to be particularly offensive.

CAREER	Attached to the Earl of Nottingham's theatrical company.
1587	Wrote *Tamburlaine the Great*. Its use of blank verse set the pattern for the Elizabethan tragedies that followed.
1588	Wrote *The Jew of Malta*.

I count religion but a childish toy,
And hold there is no sin but ignorance.

The Jew of Malta, Prologue

BARNADINE: Thou hast committed –
BARABAS: Fornication? But that was in another country: and
besides, the wench is dead.

The Jew of Malta, Act IV, sc. 1

1589	Involved in street fight in which a man was killed.
1592	Deported from the Netherlands for trying to issue forged gold coins.
1593	Wrote *Edward II*.
1593	Wrote the song 'The Passionate Shepherd to his Love'.

> Come live with me, and be my love,
> And we will all the pleasures prove,
> That valleys, groves, hills and fields,
> Woods or steepy mountains yields.
>
> 'The Passionate Shepherd to his Love'

1593	Wrote *Doctor Faustus*.
1593	Warrant issued for his arrest for propagating atheist opinions.

> It lies not in our power to love, or hate,
> For will in us is over-ruled by fate.
>
> 'Hero and Leander', first sestiad, l. 167, 1598

> Was this the face that launched a thousand ships,
> And burnt the topless towers of Ilium?
> Sweet Helen, make me immortal with a kiss!
>
> *Doctor Faustus*, Act V, sc. 1

DEATH	1593, aged 29, Deptford, East London. Stabbed in a tavern brawl, assumed murdered.
HOBBIES & INTERESTS	Money.

William Shakespeare

England's greatest playwright and poet, who has been translated into over 100 languages. He wrote directly for his own theatre companies, their performance being the first publication.

BIRTH
1564, Stratford-upon-Avon, traditionally on St George's Day (23 April), eldest son of an alderman and sometime butcher, glover and cloth dealer.

MARITAL STATUS
Married, 1582, Anne Hathaway. Two daughters, Susanna and Judith, and one son, Hamnet.

EDUCATION
King Edward VI Grammar School, Stratford.

A Little Bit of Background

Shakespeare was patronised by both Elizabeth I, who reigned 1558–1603, and James I, 1603–25. Cervantes published *Don Quixote* in 1605, the year of the Gunpowder Plot.

CAREER

1577 Worked for his father, then a butcher.

1582 Married Anne Hathaway, who was about seven years his senior, 'on account of her pregnancy'.

1583 His daughter, Susanna, was born.

1585 Left Stratford to escape prosecution for poaching. Schoolmaster.

1586 His father in debt and deprived of his alderman's gown. Moved to London.

1587 Member of the Earl of Leicester's theatre company.

1588 The company came under the patronage of first Lord Strange, then Earl Derby and then Henry Carey. In 1603, it became the King's Company of Players. The players performed in the theatres The Rose, Curtains, The Blackfriars and The Globe, which opened in 1599.

1591	Wrote *Love Labour's Lost*, *Two Gentlemen of Verona*, *The Comedy of Errors* and *Romeo and Juliet*.
1591–4	Wrote his Sonnets, which were private poems for a circle of friends.
1592	Acted in *Henry VI*.
1593	Published the epic love poem *Venus and Adonis*.
1594	Published *Titus Andronicus* and *The Merchant of Venice*.

> If you prick us, do we not bleed? If you tickle us, do we not laugh?
> If you poison us, do we not die? And if you wrong us, shall we not
> revenge? *The Merchant of Venice*, Act III, sc. 1

	Wrote *King John* and *The Rape of Lucrece*.
	Acted at Court.
1595	Wrote *A Midsummer Night's Dream* and *All's Well that Ends Well*.
1596	Published *The Taming of the Shrew*.
1597	Returned to Stratford, paid his family's debts and bought New Place, the largest house in town.
	Published *Richard II* and *Richard III*.

> This royal throne of kings, this sceptred isle,
> This earth of majesty, this seat of Mars,
> This other Eden, demi-paradise,
> This fortress built by Nature for herself
> Against infection and the hand of war,
> This happy breed of men, this little world,
> This precious stone set in the silver sea,
> Which serves it in the office of a wall,
> Or as a moat defensive to a house,
> Against the envy of less happier lands;
> This blessed plot, this earth, this realm, this England,
> This nurse, this teeming womb of royal kings,
> Fear'd by their breed, and famous by their birth. . .
> *Richard II*, Act II, sc. 1

> Now is the winter of our discontent
> Made glorious summer by this son of York.
>
> *Richard III*, Act I, sc. 1

1597 Wrote *Henry IV Parts I* and *II*, *Henry V* and *The Merry Wives of Windsor*.

1598 Acted in Ben Jonson's *Every Man in his Humour*.

1599 Wrote *Much Ado about Nothing* and *As You Like It*.

> All the world's a stage,
> And all the men and women merely players;
> They have their exits and their entrances;
> And one man in his time plays many parts,
> His acts being seven ages.
>
> *As You Like It*, Act II, sc. 7

1599 Wrote *Twelfth Night*.

> If music be the food of love, play on,
> Give me excess of it, that, surfeiting,
> The appetite may sicken and so die.
>
> *Twelfth Night*, Act I, sc. 1

1601 Produced *Julius Caesar*.

> Friends, Romans, countrymen, lend me your ears:
> I come to bury Caesar, not to praise him.
> The evil that men do lives after them;
> The good is oft interred with their bones.
>
> *Julius Caesar*, Act III, sc. 2

1602 Produced *Hamlet*.

Neither a borrower nor a lender be;
For loan oft loses both itself and friend,
And borrowing dulls the edge of husbandry.
This above all: to thine own self be true,
And it must follow, as the night the day,
Thou canst not then be false to any man.

Hamlet, Act I, sc. 3

To be, or not to be — that is the question;
Whether 'tis nobler in the mind to suffer
The slings and arrows of outrageous fortune,
Or to take arms against a sea of troubles,
And by opposing end them? To die, to sleep —
No more; and by a sleep to say we end
The heart-ache and the thousand natural shocks
That flesh is heir to, 'tis a consummation
Devoutly to be wish'd. To die, to sleep;
To sleep, perchance to dream. Ay, there's the rub;
For in that sleep of death what dreams may come,
When we have shuffled off this mortal coil,
Must give us pause.

Ibid., Act III, sc. 1

1603 Wrote *Troilus and Cressida*.
Acted in Ben Jonson's *Sejanus*.
1604 *Othello* and *Measure for Measure* performed.
1606 Finished *Macbeth*.

Is this a dagger which I see before me,
The handle toward my hand? Come, let me clutch thee:
I have thee not, and yet I see thee still.

Macbeth, Act II, sc. 1

Wrote *King Lear*.

> Get thee glass eyes
> And, like a scurvy politician, seem
> To see the things thou dost not.
>
> *King Lear*, Act IV, sc. 6

| 1607 | Wrote *Timon of Athens* and *Pericles*. |
| 1608 | Wrote *Antony and Cleopatra* and *Coriolanus*. |

> The barge she sat in, like a burnish'd throne,
> Burn'd on the water. The poop was beaten gold;
> Purple the sails, and so perfumed that
> The winds were love-sick with them; the oars were silver,
> Which to the tune of flutes kept stroke and made
> The water which they beat to follow faster,
> As amorous of their strokes. For her own person,
> It beggar'd all description.
>
> *Antony and Cleopatra*, Act II, sc. 2

1610	Wrote *Cymbeline*.
1611	Wrote *A Winter's Tale* and *The Tempest*.
1611–16	In Stratford.
1614	Last visit to London. Unsuccessfully attempted to enclose Stratford Common.
DEATH	1616, aged 52 on St George's Day, having drafted his will (leaving his wife his second-best bed) and entertained Ben Jonson. Buried in Holy Trinity Church, Stratford-upon-Avon.
HOBBIES & INTERESTS	History and property.

King James VI/I

King of Scotland from 1567 and of England 1603–25,
he united the two crowns and presided over the production
of the Authorised Version of the Bible. He was dubbed 'the
wisest fool in Christendom' by Henry IV of France.

BIRTH | 1566, at Edinburgh Castle, son of Mary Queen of Scots and
Lord Darnley.

MARITAL | Married, 1589, Anne of Denmark, in Norway. Three sons,
Henry, Prince of Wales (d. 1612), Charles (later Charles I) and
Robert, Duke of Kintyre and Lorne. Four daughters,
Elizabeth, Margaret, Mary and Sophia.

EDUCATION | Tutored by George Buchanan, Scottish humanist and
reformer.

 ## A Little Bit of Background

Galileo perfected his telescope in 1609. The Thirty Years' War,
an intermittent power struggle between the kings of France and the
Habsburg rulers of the Holy Roman Empire and Spain, began in 1618. In
1619, slaves from Africa reached Virginia, and, a year later, in 1620, the
Pilgrim Fathers departed from Plymouth for New England.

CAREER

1567 | Crowned King of Scotland, aged one, following his mother's
abdication.

1582 | Kidnapped by Protestant nobles.

1583 | Escaped.

1584 | Drove the rebellious Protestant nobles out of Scotland.

1586 | Accepted a pension from Elizabeth I, despite appealing for
clemency on behalf of his mother.
Disinherited by his mother in favour of Philip II of Spain.

1587 | His mother, Mary Queen of Scots, executed by Elizabeth I.

1589	Married Anne of Denmark.
1599	Published *Basilikon Doron*, in which he expounded the theory of the divine right of kings.
1603	Crowned King of England.
	Published *True Lawe of Free Monarchies*.
1604	Made peace with Rome. Imprisoned Sir Walter Ralegh.

A branch of the sin of drunkenness, which is the root of all sins.

A Counterblast to Tobacco, 1604

A custom loathsome to the eye, hateful to the nose, harmful to the brain, dangerous to the lungs, and in the black, stinking fume thereof, nearest resembling the horrible Stygian smoke of the pit that is bottomless. Ibid.

No bishop, no King. *Sum and Substance of the Conference*, W. Barlow, 1604

1605	The Gunpowder Plot.
1607	Published *Apology for the Oath of Allegiance*.
1608	Allied with the Dutch.
1611	Created the title of Baronet – to sell.
1611	Issued the Authorised or King James Version of the Bible.
	Dissolved his first Parliament.
1614	Dissolved his second Parliament and imprisoned four members.

'The state of monarchy is the supremest thing upon earth; for kings are not only God's lieutenants upon earth, and sit upon God's throne, but even by God himself they are called gods.'

Speech to Parliament, 21 March 1610, in Works, 1616

1618	Executed Ralegh to mollify the Spaniards.
1622	Dissolved his third Parliament and penalised the leaders.
DEATH	1625, aged 58. Buried in Westminster Abbey.
HOBBIES & INTERESTS	Thwarting smokers.

Oliver Cromwell

English parliamentarian, soldier and statesman who created the New Model Army and, as Lord Protector, ruled 1653–8, but refused the crown.

BIRTH	1599, in Huntingdon.
MARITAL STATUS	Married, 1620, Elizabeth Bourchier. Five sons, Robert, Oliver, Richard (Lord Protector 1658–9), Henry and James. Four daughters, Bridget, Elizabeth, Mary and Frances.
EDUCATION	Sidney Sussex College, Cambridge.

 ## A Little Bit of Background

The causes of the English Civil War, which raged from 1642 to 1689, were partly religious and partly political. Supporters of Charles I were known as Cavaliers, those of Parliament as Roundheads. The immediate cause of the conflict was the refusal of the Long Parliament (called by Charles in 1640) to meet the demands put upon it by the King. After the mayhem of the Civil War, Cromwell restored England's reputation abroad and imposed order where there had been uncertainty and chaos. His ruthlessness, efficiency, soberness and practicality were a stark contrast to the wilfulness and flamboyance of both Charles I and his son, Charles II.

CAREER	
c. **1617**	Entered Lincoln's Inn.
1628	MP for Huntingdon.
1630	JP for Huntingdon.
1638	Underwent a religious 'renewal'.
1640	MP for Cambridge.
1642	Fought in Essex's Army at Edgehill.
1643	Converted his troop of horse into a regiment.
	Suppressed royalists at Lowestoft.
	Recaptured Stamford.

| 1643 | Governor of the Isle of Ely. |

A few honest men are better than numbers.

Letter to William Spring, September 1643, *Oliver Cromwell's Letters and Speeches*,
Thomas Carlyle, 2nd ed., 1846

I would rather have a plain russet-coated captain that knows what he fights for, and loves what he knows, than that which you call 'a gentleman' and is nothing else.

Ibid.

| 1644 | Lieutenant General.
Commanded the left wing at Marston Moor. |

God made them as stubble to our swords.   Ibid.

1645	Helped remodel army. Relieved Taunton. Successful at Naseby.
1647	Sympathetic to the Army's grievance with Parliament.
1648	Crushed Welsh insurrection. Crushed the Scots at Preston.
1649	President of the Council of State after Charles I's execution.

'Cruel necessity.'

On the execution of Charles I, quoted in *Anecdotes*,
Joseph Spence, 1820

| 1649 | Commander-in-Chief and Lord Lieutenant of Ireland. |

Hell or Connaught.

Traditionally attributed summary of the choice offered to the Catholic
population of Ireland, who were transported to the western
counties to make room for settlers

Stormed Drogheda and Wexford and massacred the garrisons.

It has pleased God to bless our endeavours at Drogheda . . . I believe we put to the sword the whole number of the defendants.

Letter to Bradshaw, September 1649

1650 Returned to England.

I beseech you, in the bowels of Christ, think it possible you may be mistaken.

Letter to the General Assembly of the Kirk of Scotland, 3 August 1650,
Oliver Cromwell's Letters and Speeches, Thomas Carlyle, 1845

Defeated the Scots at Dunbar.
1651 Defeated the Scots at Worcester.
1653 Lord Protector and Head of State.

'You have been sat too long here for any good you have been doing. Depart, I say, and let us have done with you. In the name of God, go!'

Addressing the Rump Parliament, 20 April 1653, oral tradition,
Memorials of the English Affairs, Bulstrode Whitelock, 1732 ed.

'Take away the fool's bauble, the mace.'

At the dismissal of the Rump Parliament, 20 April 1653, ibid.

1654 Made peace with the Dutch, and signed treaties with Sweden, Denmark and Portugal.

'It's a maxim not to be despised. "Though peace be made, yet it's interest that keeps peace"'

Speech to Parliament, 4 September 1654,
Oliver Cromwell's Letters and Speeches, Thomas Carlyle, 1845

'Necessity hath no law. Feigned necessities, imaginary necessities . . . are the greatest cozenage that men can put upon the Providence of God, and make pretences to break known rules by.'

Speech to Parliament, 12 September 1654,
ibid.

1655	Divided the country under 12 major generals.
	Prohibited the use of the *Book of Common Prayer*.
1656	Invited the Jews to return.
1657	Refused title of King.

Mr Lely, I desire you would use all your skill to paint my picture truly like me, and not flatter me at all; but remark all these roughnesses, pimples, warts and everything as you see me; otherwise I will never pay a farthing for it.

Instructions to Lely, the Court painter

'Your poor army, those poor contemptible men, came up hither.'

Speech to Parliament, 21 April 1657, *Oliver Cromwell's Letters and Speeches*, Thomas Carlyle, 1845

1658	Defeated the Spaniards at Dunkirk.

'You have accounted yourselves happy on being environed with a great ditch from all the world besides.'

Speech to Parliament, 21 April 1657, ibid.

DEATH	1658, aged 59, of malaria. Buried in Westminster Abbey, but exhumed in 1661 and posthumously hanged, drawn and quartered and hung on the gallows at Tyburn.
HOBBIES & INTERESTS	Farming.

King Charles I

Cultured but autocratic King of England, Scotland and Ireland 1625–49, whose insensitivity and impatience with Parliament eventually cost him his head.

BIRTH	1600, at Dunfermline Palace, second son of James I (then James IV of Scotland) and Anne of Denmark.
MARITAL STATUS	Married, 1625, Princess Henrietta Maria of France (by Proxy). Four sons, Charles James (died at birth), Henry, Charles (later Charles II) and James (later James II). Five daughters, Mary, Elizabeth, Anne, Catherine and Henrietta.
EDUCATION	At Court.

CAREER

1604	Came to England.
1612	Became heir apparent when his brother, Henry, died.
1616	Made Prince of Wales.
1625	Married Henrietta Maria and succeeded to the throne. Dissolved his first Parliament.
1626	Dissolved his second Parliament.
1626–9	War with France.
1628	His third Parliament forced him to sign The Petition of Right.
1629	Dissolved his third Parliament.
1629–40	Governed without Parliament.

A Little Bit of Background

In 1628, William Harvey demonstrated the circulation of the blood. In France, Cardinal Richelieu was starving the French Protestants into submission. Louis XIV became King of France in 1643. In 1639, Holland suffered the Tulip Crash when the bottom fell out of the tulip market.

1629–40	Raised funds by 'ship money', a tax originally levied on coastal property in times of war, but which he applied during peace and extended inland. By so doing, he hoped to avoid having to summon Parliament, whose right it was to control revenue.
1633	Crowned in Scotland, offending the Calvinist Scots with his use of 'Roman Rites'.

Never make a defence or apology before you be accused.

Letter to Lord Wentworth, 3 September 1636, *Letters of King Charles I*, ed. Sir Charles Petrie, 1935

1637	Caused riots in Scotland by imposition of the High Church liturgy devised by Archbishop Laud.
1639	Invaded Scotland, but forced to sign Treaty of Berwick.
1640	Called and dissolved fourth Parliament (which he intended to supply him with funds to punish the Scots).
	Scots occupied Newcastle and Durham, and were invited to cross the Tweed by Parliament.
	Called fifth Parliament (The Long Parliament).
1641	Assented (to his deep shame) to the execution of Strafford.
	Went to Scotland for help against 'extremists'.
	Appealed for help to Irish Catholic lords.
	Returned to London
1642	Tried to arrest 'five members' of Parliament.

'I see all the birds are flown.'

After attempting to arrest five members of the Long Parliament (Pym, Hampden, Haselrig, Holles and Strode) in the House of Commons, 4 January 1642

	The Battle of Edgehill.

'Your King is your Cause, your Quarrel and your Captain.'

Charles's speech before the Battle of Edgehill

	Declared war at Nottingham.
1645	Army crushed at Naseby.

1646	Surrendered to Scots at Newark.
1647	Fled to the Isle of Wight.
1649	Refused to plead at his trial, denying that a king could be legally tried by such a court, and was condemned.

'As to the King, the laws of the land will clearly instruct you for that . . . for the people; and truly I desire their liberty and freedom, as much as any body: but I must tell you, that their liberty and freedom consists in having the government of those laws, by which their life and their goods may be most their own; 'tis not for having share in government [sirs] that is nothing pertaining to 'em. A subject and a sovereign are clean different things.'

Speech on the scaffold, 30 January 1649, *Historical Collections*, J. Rushworth, pt 4, vol. 2, 1701

'I die a Christian, according to the profession of the Church of England, as I found it left me by my father.'

Ibid.

| **DEATH** | 1649, aged 48, beheaded outside Banqueting House, Palace of Whitehall. Buried in St George's Chapel, Windsor. |
| **HOBBIES & INTERESTS** | Art. |

John Milton

Puritan poet and author of the epic poem Paradise Lost, *in which he tried to 'justify the ways of God to men'. A staunch parliamentarian, Milton lived under the rule of three Stuart kings and Oliver Cromwell.*

BIRTH	1608, Bread Street, Cheapside, London, the son of a scrivener.
MARITAL STATUS	Married three times: *i* 1643, Mary Powell, d. 1652, three daughters, Anne, Mary and Deborah, and one son, John, who died in infancy; *ii* 1656, Catherine Woodcock, d. 1658, one daughter, Katherine; *iii* 1662, Elizabeth Minshull.
EDUCATION	St Paul's School, London, and Christ's College, Cambridge, where he was know as the Lady of Christ's for his 'womanly form and dainty ways'.

CAREER

1629	Wrote 'Nativity Ode'.
1630	Wrote 'On Shakespeare'.
1632–8	Lived with his father.
1632	Wrote 'L'Allegro' and 'Il Penseroso'.
1633	Wrote 'Arcades'.
1634	Wrote *Comus*.
1637	Wrote *Lycidas*.
1637–9	Travelled in Italy and Europe.

 A Little Bit of Background

The Authorised Version of the Bible was issued in 1611. Shakespeare died in 1616. Charles I came to the throne in 1625 and was executed after seven years of civil war in 1649. Cromwell was Lord Protector from 1653 to 1658. Charles II was crowned in 1660.

1639–47	Tutored his two nephews and others.
1641	Published pamphlets attacking bishops.
1643	Relinquished his ambitions to become a minister and married a woman half his age, Mary Powell, who fled back to her father after only one month of marriage.
	Published a pamphlet on *The Doctrine and Discipline of Divorce*.

> Let not England forget her precedence of teaching nations how to live.
>
> *The Doctrine and Discipline of Divorce*,
> 'To the Parliament of England', 1643

1644	Published *The Judgement of Martin Bucer on Divorce*. Wrote *Areopagitica*. Became aware he was losing his sight.

> Give me the liberty to know, to utter, and to argue freely according to conscience, above all liberties.
>
> *Areopagitica*, 1644

1645	His wife returns.

> Let us with a gladsome mind
> Praise the Lord, for he is kind,
> For his mercies ay endure,
> Ever faithful, ever sure.
>
> 'Let us with a gladsome mind', 1645

1647	Began his *History of Britain* (published 1669).

> For what can war, but endless war still breed?
>
> On the Lord General Fairfax, at the Siege of Colchester, 1648

1649	Published *The Tenure of Kings And Magistrates*, following Charles I's execution.
1649–60	Secretary to the Council of State.
1650	Began *Paradise Lost* (finished 1663) and sold copyright for £10.

1652	Totally blind. Wife died.
1656	Married Catherine Woodcock, who died 1658.
1660	Went into hiding on the Restoration of Charles II.
1662	Married Elizabeth Minshull.

> Of man's first disobedience, and the fruit
> Of that forbidden tree, whose mortal taste
> Brought death into the world, and all our woe,
> With loss of Eden.
>
> *Paradise Lost*, bk 1, l. 1
>
> What though the field be lost?
> All is not lost; the unconquerable will,
> And study of revenge, immortal hate,
> And courage never to submit or yield.
>
> Ibid., bk 1, l. 105

1671	Published *Paradise Regained* and *Samson Agonistes*.

> Doth God exact day-labour, light denied,
> I fondly ask; but patience to prevent
> That murmur, soon replies, God doth not need
> Either man's work or his own gifts, who best
> Bear his mild yoke, they serve him best, his state
> Is kingly. Thousands at his bidding speed
> And post o'er land and ocean without rest:
> They also serve who only stand and wait.
>
> Sonnet 16, 'When I consider how my light is spent', 1673

DEATH	1674, aged 65, from gout. Buried in St Giles's Church without Cripplegate, London Wall.
HOBBIES & INTERESTS	The Bible.

George Fox

English founder of the Society of Friends, commonly known as the Quakers. He preached that each man should listen to God within himself and was frequently imprisoned for his beliefs.

BIRTH | 1624, in Fenny Drayton, Leicestershire.

MARITAL STATUS | Married, 1669, Margaret Fell, a widow, one of his earliest followers.

EDUCATION | Village school.

A Little Bit of Background

Charles I was executed in 1649. The Commonwealth lasted until 1660, when the monarchy was restored and Charles II became king. Charles's successor, his Catholic brother James II, who came to the throne in 1685, was ousted by the Protestant William of Orange in 1688.

CAREER

1640 | Agent to a wool dealer.

1643 | Left Leicestershire and went south.

1644–6 | Travelled the countryside questioning clergy about their faith.

1647–8 | Preached.

> I saw also that there was an ocean of darkness and death, but an infinite ocean of light and love, which flowed over the ocean of darkness.
>
> *Journal*, 1647

1649 | Imprisoned for brawling in a church.
Founded the Society of the Friends of Truth.

1650	The Society nicknamed 'Quakers', a reference to their fits of ecstasy, by Gervase Bennet.

> Walk cheerfully over the world, answering that of God in every one.
>
> Ibid., 1656

1657	Visited Scotland.

> All bloody principles and practices, we, as to our own particulars, do utterly deny, with all outward wars and strife and fightings with outward weapons, for any end or under any pretence whatsoever. And this is our testimony to the whole world.
>
> Ibid., 1661

1663–6	Imprisoned first in Lancaster and then in Scarborough.
1669	First Yearly Meeting of the Society. Visited Ireland.
1671–2	Visited America and the West Indies.
1673–4	Imprisoned in Worcester.
1677–84	Visited Holland.
1694	His *Journal* published posthumously.
DEATH	1691, aged 66. He was buried in Bunhill Field Burial Ground, City Road, London, though his grave is no longer identifiable due to bomb damage.
HOBBIES & INTERESTS	Salvation.

John Bunyan

*English writer and Non-conformist preacher who fought
with the Parliamentary Army, spent much of his life in
prison, and wrote* The Pilgrim's Progress, *a religious
allegory which tells how Christian, a pilgrim, sets off with
the burden of sins on his back to make his way to the
Celestial City.*

BIRTH	1628, Elstow, near Bedford, son of a tinsmith.
MARITAL STATUS	Married first, *c.* 1650, Mary, d. *c.* 1656. Two daughters, Mary (born blind) and Elizabeth, and two sons, John and Thomas. Secondly, *c.* 1659, Elizabeth, d. 1691.
EDUCATION	Village school.

 ## A Little Bit of Background

England underwent a civil war between 1642–9 and, after the execution of Charles I, became a republic between 1649–60. Charles II's reign, 1660–85, included the Plague and the Great Fire of London. The brief reign of his brother, James II, a Catholic, was interrupted by the Duke of Monmouth's rebellion and ended by the Glorious Revolution of 1688, which placed the Protestants William and Mary on the throne.

CAREER	Initially assisted his father, mending pots and pans. Enlisted with the Parliamentary forces to spite his father, who had remarried on the death of his mother.
1644–6	Stationed at Newport Pagnell. Wracked with guilt and remorse at the death of a fellow soldier, shot while covering his absence without leave.
1653	Joined Mr Gifford's Church in Bedford.
1655	Appointed a deacon and began to preach.
1656	On the death of his wife, published *Some Gospel Truths Opened.*

1657	Published *A Vindication*, attacking the Quakers. Preached throughout Bedfordshire.
1660	Arrested for preaching without a licence.
1661–72	Imprisoned for his refusal to deny his 'intention to preach'.
	Earned a living in prison by making tagged laces.
	Wrote nine books.
1675	Re-imprisoned.
	On his release, wrote *The Pilgrim's Progress*.
1678	The first part of *The Pilgrim's Progress* is published.

> As I walked through the wilderness of this world.
>
> Opening words, *The Pilgrim's Progress*, Pt 1, 1678

> It is an hard matter for a man to go down into the valley of Humiliation . . . and to catch no slip by the way.
>
> *The Pilgrim's Progress*, Pt. 1, 1678

> It beareth the name of Vanity-Fair, because the town where 'tis kept, is lighter than vanity.
>
> Ibid.

> Then I saw that there was a way to Hell, even from the gates of heaven.
>
> Ibid.

1684	The second part of *The Pilgrim's Progress* is published.

> He that is down needs fear no fall,
> He that is low no pride,
> He that is humble ever shall
> Have God to be his guide.
>
> 'Shepherd Boy's Song', *The Pilgrim's Progress*, Pt 2, 1684

Who would true valour see,
Let him come hither,
One here will constant be,
Come wind, come weather.
There's no discouragement
Shall make him once relent
His first avowed intent
To be a pilgrim.

So he passed over, and the trumpets sounded for
him on the other side.

The Pilgrim's Progress, Pt 2, 1684

DEATH | 1688, aged 59, of a fever resulting from a cold. Buried in Bunhill Fields, London.

HOBBIES & INTERESTS | Preaching.

King Charles II

King of England, Scotland and Ireland 1660–85, who restored the monarchy after the Commonwealth. His reign, which was noted for its licentiousness, was in part a reaction to the drab years that had preceded it.

BIRTH	1630, in St James's Palace, London, second son of Charles I.
MARITAL STATUS	Married, 1662, Catherine of Braganza. Had at least 13 official mistresses and many illegitimate children, including a son, the Duke of Monmouth.
EDUCATION	At Court.

A Little Bit of Background

The Royal Society (Britain's oldest scientific society) was founded in 1660, and the final version of the *Book of Common Prayer* was issued in 1662. The last great Plague struck in 1665, and was followed by the Great Fire of London a year later. The Habeas Corpus Act, requiring a person who detains another to produce his prisoner in court, was passed in 1679.

CAREER	
1638	Made Prince of Wales.
1640	Took his seat in the House of Lords.
1646	Defied Fairfax in Devon and Cornwall.
Mar	Retreated to the Scilly Isles.
Apr	Retreated to Jersey.
July	Fled to Paris.
1649	Proclaimed King in Edinburgh.
1650	Agreed to the terms of the Scots and took up residence in Fife.
1650	Defeated at Dunbar.
1651	Crowned at Scone in Scotland.

1651	Beaten at Worcester.
1651–4	Lived in poverty in Paris.
1656	Set up his court in Bruges.
	Excluded from the succession by Act of Parliament.
1658	Set up his court in Brussels.
1659	Negotiated with General Monck about his restoration.
1660	Proclaimed King in London.

> Here lies our Sovereign Lord the King
> Whose word no man relies on;
> He never said a foolish thing,
> Nor ever did a wise one.
>
> Earl of Rochester's proposed epitaph to Charles II
>
> 'This is very true: for my words are my own, and my actions are my ministers.'
>
> Charles's reply to Lord Rochester's suggestion, *Remarks and Collections*, Thomas Hearne, 1885–1921, 17 November 1706

1661	Crowned.
	Secretly allied himself to Louis XIV of France.
1662	Married Catherine of Braganza.
1662	Sold Dunkirk and Mardyke to France.
1663	Made his illegitimate son, born to his mistress Lucy Walter during his exile in Holland, Duke of Monmouth.

> He [Charles II] said once to myself, he was no atheist, but he could not think God would make a man miserable only for taking a little pleasure out of the way.
>
> *History of My Own Time*, Bishop Gilbert Burnet, vol. 1, bk 2, 1724

1666	Distinguished himself fighting the Great Fire of London.

> It is upon the navy under the good Providence of God that the safety, honour, and welfare of this realm do chiefly depend.
>
> Articles of War, preamble (probably a popular paraphrase), *The Naval Side of British History*, Geoffrey Callender, pt 1, ch. 8, 1952

1667	Dutch destroyed fleet in the Medway.
1668	Agreed to the Triple Alliance with Sweden and Holland.
1670	Signed secret Treaty of Dover with Louis XIV.

> 'I am sure no man in England will take away my life to make you King.'
>
> To his brother James, *Political & Literary Anecdotes*, William King, 1818

1682	Laid the foundation stone of Chelsea Hospital, London.

> 'I am weary of travelling and am resolved to go abroad no more. But when I am dead and gone I know not what my brother will do: I am much afraid that when he comes to wear the crown he will be obliged to travel again.'
>
> On the difference between himself and his brother (later James II), attributed

DEATH	1685, aged 54, from a stroke. He converted to Roman Catholicism on his deathbed. Buried at Westminster Abbey.

> 'Let not poor Nelly starve.'
>
> Reputedly his last words, of his mistress, Nell Gwyn

HOBBIES & INTERESTS	Chemistry, naval architecture, horses and women.

John Locke

*English philosopher, described by John Stuart Mill as
the founder of analytical philosophy, whose writings had
a profound influence on the authors of the American
Declaration of Independence.*

BIRTH	1632, in Wrington, Somerset.
MARITAL STATUS	Single.
EDUCATION	Westminster School and Christ Church, Oxford.

CAREER

1660	Lecturer in Greek at Oxford.
1662	Lecturer on Rhetoric at Oxford.
1663	Censor of Moral Philosophy at Oxford.
1667	Wrote *An Essay concerning Human Understanding*.
1668	Successfully operated on an abscess on the chest of Parliamentarian Anthony Ashley Cooper.
	Fellow of the Royal Society (FRS).
1675	Bachelor of Medicine.
1669–72	Secretary to the Lords Proprietors of Carolina.

 ## A Little Bit of Background

England underwent a civil war between 1642 and 1649, when Charles I was executed and England became a republic. The monarchy was restored under Charles II, who reigned 1660–85. He was succeeded by his brother, James II, a Catholic, whose brief reign was interrupted by the Duke of Monmouth's rebellion and ended by the Glorious Revolution of 1688, which placed Protestants William and Mary on the throne. Isaac Newton published *Principia Mathematica* in 1607. Edward Lloyd opened his insurance coffee shop in 1692 and the Bank of England was founded in 1694.

1672	Secretary of Presentations under the Lord Chancellor.
1673–5	Secretary to the Council of Trade.
1675–9	In France.
1679–84	In Oxford.
1685–9	In Holland, where he met William, Prince of Orange.
1689–1704	Commissioner of Appeal.
1689	Published *Letter* on Toleration in Latin, then English.
1690	Published *An Essay Concerning Human Understanding*.

New opinions are always suspected, and usually opposed, without any other reason but because they are not already common.

An Essay concerning Human Understanding, 'Dedicatory Epistle'

Nature never makes excellent things for mean or no uses.

Ibid., bk 1 ch. 1, sect. 15

No man's knowledge here can go beyond his experience.

Ibid., bk 2, ch. 1, sect. 19

It is one thing to show a man that he is in error, and another to put him in possession of truth.

Ibid., bk 4, ch. 7, sect. 11

Published second *Letter* on Toleration and *Two Treatises of Government*.

. . . the end of law is, not to abolish or restrain, but to preserve and enlarge freedom.

Second Treatise of Civil Government, ch. 6, sect. 57

The great and chief end, therefore, of men's uniting into commonwealths, and putting themselves under government, is the preservation of their property.

Ibid., ch. 9, sect. 124

1691	Lived in Essex.
1692	Published third *Letter* on Toleration.
1693	Published treatise *On Education*.

1695	Published treatise on the *Reasonableness of Christianity*. Published treatise on *Currency*.

> The rod, which is the only instrument of government that tutors generally know, or ever think of, is the most unfit of any to be used in education.
>
> *Some Thoughts concerning Education*, sect. 47, 5th ed., 1705
>
> You would think him a very foolish fellow, that should not value a virtuous, or a wise man, infinitely before a great scholar.
>
> Ibid., sect. 147, 5th ed., 1705

1696–1700	Member of the Council of Trade.
1705–7	*Paraphrases of St Paul's Epistle* published posthumously.
DEATH	1704, aged 72, at the house of Lady Masham, an admirer, in Oates, Essex. Buried in All Saints' Churchyard, High Laver, Essex.
HOBBIES & INTERESTS	Ancient Greek and medicine.

Sir Christopher Wren

Architect of St Paul's Cathedral and many churches and chapels — 52 in London alone — who is known as 'The British Poet Laureate of Architecture'.

BIRTH | 1632, at East Knoyle, son of the Dean of Windsor.

MARITAL STATUS | Married first, 1669, Faith Coghill, d. 1675. Two sons, Gilbert and Christopher. Secondly, 1677, Jane Fitzwilliam, d. 1679. One daughter, Jane, and one son, William.

EDUCATION | Westminster School and Wadham College, Oxford.

CAREER

1653–61	Fellow of All Souls' College, Oxford.
1657–61	Professor of Astronomy, Gresham College, London.
1661–73	Professor of Astronomy, Oxford.
1660	Drew up preamble of the Charter of the Royal Society.
1663	Became interested in Architecture and assisted the Surveyor-General to the Royal Works.
	Built Pembroke College Chapel, Cambridge.
1664–9	Built Sheldonian Theatre, Oxford.
1666/7	Appointed Surveyor-General and Principal Architect for rebuilding the City of London after the Great Fire.
1668	Built Emmanuel College Chapel, Cambridge.
	Appointed to pull down and rebuild St Paul's Cathedral, London.

Architecture has its political use; public buildings being the ornament of a country; it establishes a nation, draws people and commerce; makes the people love their native country, which passion is the original of all great actions in a commonwealth.

Parentalia, or Memories of the family of the Wrens, Christopher Wren, 1750

1669–1718	Surveyor-General to the Royal Works.
1670–1722	Built 52 churches and chapels in London.

1671–8	Designed and built the Monument, erected to commemorate the Great Fire of London.
1673	Completed the design of St Paul's, which continued to evolve as it was built.
1677–92	Designed and built the Library of Trinity College, Cambridge.
1681–2	President of the Royal Society.
1682	Designed and built the Chelsea Hospital, London.
1684	Comptroller of Works at Windsor Castle.
1685	MP for Plympton.
1689	MP for Windsor.
1698	Surveyor to Westminster Abbey.
1701	MP for Weymouth.
1716	St Paul's Cathedral completed.
DEATH	1723, aged 90. Buried in St Paul's Cathedral.

> *Lector, si monumentum requiris, circumspice*
> (Reader, if you seek his memorial, look around you)
>
> Inscription on Wren's tomb

HOBBIES & INTERESTS	Barometers, anatomy and medicine.

Sir Isaac Newton

English mathematician and physicist, who identified the force of gravity and was arguably the greatest scientist who has ever lived, but who was knighted for his work at the Royal Mint.

BIRTH	1642, at Woolsthorpe Manor, Lincolnshire.
MARITAL STATUS	Single. His sweetheart, Anne Storey, married another.
EDUCATION	Grantham Grammar School and Trinity College, Cambridge.

CAREER

1665	Awarded a Bachelor of Arts.
1666	Left Cambridge to escape the Plague and, while in the garden at Woolsthorpe, came up with the idea of Universal Gravitation. Also discovered the binomial theorem, integral and differential calculus, and computed the area of the hyperbola.
1667	Fellow of Trinity College, Cambridge. Concentrated on optics.
1668	Built a reflecting telescope.
1669	Elected Lucasian Professor of Mathematics, Cambridge.
1671	Presented his second reflecting telescope to the Royal Society.
1672	Fellow of the Royal Society (FRS). Read out his *New Theory about Light and Colours*.

If I have seen further it is by standing on the shoulders of giants.

Letter to Robert Hooke, 5 February 1676, *Correspondence of Isaac Newton*, vol. 1, ed. H.W. Turnbull, 1959

1687	Published *Philosophiae Naturalis Principia Mathematica*.

Every body continues in its state of rest, or of uniform motion in a right line, unless it is compelled to change that state by forces impressed upon it.

Principia Mathematica, Laws of Motion I, 1687, translated by Andrew Motte, 1729

To every action there is always opposed an equal reaction.

Ibid., Laws of Motion 3

1689	MP for Cambridge University.
1696	Warden of the Mint.
1699	Master of the Mint.
1701–02	MP for Cambridge University.
1703–28	President of the Royal Society.
1704	Published *Opticks*.

The changing of bodies into light, and light into bodies, is very conformable to the course of Nature, which seems delighted with transmutations.

Opticks, Bk 3, pt 1, question 30, ed. 1730

1705	Knighted by Queen Anne.

I don't know what I may seem to the world, but as to myself, I seem to have been only like a boy playing on the sea-shore and diverting myself in now and then finding a smoother pebble or a prettier shell than ordinary, whilst the great ocean of truth lay all undiscovered before me.

Anecdotes, no. 1259, Joseph Spence, ed. J. Osborn, 1966

DEATH	1727, aged 84, at Kensington. Buried in Westminster Abbey.
HOBBIES & INTERESTS	Astronomy.

Duke of Marlborough

John Churchill, the outstanding soldier of his age, whose victory at Blenheim shattered Louis XIV's ambitions in Europe.

BIRTH	1650, Musbury, Devon.
MARITAL	Married, 1677, Sarah Jennings, close friend and confidante of Princess, later Queen, Anne. Two sons, both of whom died young, and four daughters, Harriet, Anne, Elizabeth and Mary. As he had no male heir, the law was amended to allow his title to be passed through the female line.
EDUCATION	St Paul's School, London.

A Little Bit of Background

William of Orange ousted James II in 1689, and reigned jointly with his wife, Mary, elder daughter of James, until her death in 1694, and then solely until his own death in 1702. Queen Anne, the second daughter of James II, reigned from 1702 to 1714. The War of the Spanish Succession ended in 1713. Louis XIV of France died in 1714.

CAREER	Favourite of the Duchess of Cleveland.
	Page to James, the Duke of York, the future James II.
1667	Ensign in the Foot Guards.
1672	Captain of Foot.
1672–7	Served in Flanders.
1674	Colonel in French Service.
1678	Colonel of Foot.
1678	Married Sarah Jennings, Maid of Honour to Princess Anne, the future Queen Anne.
1678	Envoy to the Prince of Orange.
1679	In Holland with the Duke of York.
1679–82	In Scotland with the Duke of York.

1682	Created Baron Churchill of Aymouth, Scotland.
1683	Colonel of 1st Dragoons.
1685	Envoy to Louis XIV of France.
	Created Baron Churchill of Sandridge.
	Crushed the Duke of Monmouth's rebellion.
	Major General and Colonel of 3rd Horse Guards.
1687	Offered support to the Prince of Orange.
1688	Lieutenant General.
	Swore loyalty to James II.
	Abandoned James for William of Orange.
1689	Created Earl of Marlborough.
	Commanded English troops in Flanders.
1690	Commander-in-Chief in England.
	Took Cork and Kinsale, Ireland.
1691	Went to Flanders with William III.
1692	Dismissed from his office for plotting with the army, and confined to the Tower.
1698	Back in favour and appointed Governor of the Duke of Gloucester.
1701	With William III in Holland.
1702	Queen Anne succeeds to the throne.
	Knight of the Order of the Garter.
1702–11	Captain General and Master General of the Ordnance.
	War with France.
	Commander of Forces in Holland.
	Took Venloo, Ruvemonde and Liege.
	Created Duke of Marlborough.
1703	Son dies.
	Took Bonn and Limburg.
1704	Took his army to Bavaria and joined Prince Eugene.
	Defeated the Bavarians and French at Blenheim.

I have not time to say more, but to beg you will give my duty to the Queen, and let her know her army has had a glorious victory. Tallard and two other generals are in my coach and I am following the rest. The bearer my aide de camp Colonel Parker will give her an account of what has passed.

Note written by Marlborough to his wife after the Battle of Blenheim, 1704

111

1705	Created Prince of Mendelheim.
	Voted Woodstock Manor and Blenheim Palace by Parliament.
	Invaded Brabant.
	Visited Vienna, Berlin and Hanover, mollifying allies.
1706	Defeated the French at Ramillies.
	Occupied Brussels, Antwerp and Ostend.
1707	Awarded a pension by Parliament.
	Visited the Elector of Hanover and the kings of Sweden and Prussia.
1708	Defeated the French at Oudenarde.
	Took Lille and Ghent.
1709	Defeated the French at Malplaquet.
	Out of favour as Queen Anne is finally provoked beyond breaking point by his wife's tantrums and his untimely application to be made Captain General for Life.

> The Duke returned from the wars today and did pleasure me three times in his top boots.
>
> The Duchess of Marlborough

1710	Attended peace conferences.
	Took Douai.
1711	Took Bouchain.
	Accused of corruption.
	Dismissed.
1713	Lost lands at Mandelheim.
1714	Wooed the Hanoverians and smoothed the succession of George I.
	Captain General and Master of the Ordnance.
1716	Suffered a stroke and 'succumbed to senile delinquency'.
DEATH	1722, aged 72. Buried at Blenheim Palace Chapel.
HOBBIES & INTERESTS	Hunting.

William of Orange

Stadholder of Holland from 1672 and King of Great Britain and Ireland from 1688, whose principal concern was the creation and maintenance of a coalition against the power of France.

BIRTH

1650, at The Hague, posthumous son of William II of Orange and Mary, daughter of Charles I.

MARITAL STATUS

Married, 1677, Mary, elder daughter of James II.

EDUCATION

At Leiden.

CAREER

1667   Admitted to Dutch Council of State.

1670   Visited England and received honorary degrees from all the universities.

1672   Captain General of Dutch forces and Stadholder

1677   Married Mary, daughter of the Duke of York, the future James II.

1678   Treaty of Nijmegen.

1681   Visited England.

1688   Accepted invitation from Parliament to come to England.
When James II fled, William and Mary were proclaimed joint King and Queen by Declaration of Right (not conquest).

1689   Crowned.
Formed Grand Alliance against the French.

A Little Bit of Background

After the vagaries of the Stuart kings, and the Civil War of 1642–9, Parliament was no longer prepared to give the monarch a free hand and insisted William signed the Bill of Rights in 1689.

1690	Went to Ireland and defeated James II's Franco-Irish army at the Battle of the Boyne.
1691	In Holland.
1693	Defeated at Landen, Holland, by Luxemburg.
1694	Queen Mary died of smallpox.
1695	Took Namur.
1697	Peace of Ryswyk.
1701	Assented to the Act of Settlement, which barred Catholics from the throne.

> 'There is one way never to see your country lost, and that is to die in the last ditch.'
>
> *History of My Own Time*, Bishop Gilbert Burnet, 1838 ed.
>
> Every bullet has its billet.
>
> *Journal*, 6 June 1765, John Wesley, 1827

DEATH	1702, aged 52. He fell from his horse when it stumbled on a molehill. Buried in Westminster Abbey.
HOBBIES & INTERESTS	Holland.

Jonathan Swift

Author, most famous for Gulliver's Travels, *a satirical account of various journeys to four fantastical lands undertaken by a ship's surgeon. Swift was also Dean of St Patrick's, Dublin.*

BIRTH	1667, in Dublin. His father died before he was born and his mother abandoned him. Brought up by his uncle.
MARITAL STATUS	May have married Esther Johnson (thought to be the 'Stella' to whom Swift addressed a series of letters, published, after his death, in 1767, as *Journal to Stella*), who he first met as an eight-year-old child when in the employ of Sir William Temple.
EDUCATION	Kilkenny Grammar School, where a fellow pupil was Congreve, and Trinity College, Dublin, where he was publicly censored for 'offences against discipline'.

 ## A Little Bit of Background

Scotland and England were united in 1707. The War of the Spanish Succession ended in 1713. The South Sea Bubble, the name given to the rapid rise in the value of the shares of the South Sea Company and others, burst in 1720, leading to the ruin of many speculators.

CAREER

1692	Secretary to Sir William Temple of Moor Park, Surrey.
1694	Ordained in Ireland and given the prebend of Kilroot.
1696	Returned to the employ of Sir William Temple.
1697	Wrote *The Battle of the Books*, a mock-heroic account of a struggle between classical and modern authors, and *A Tale of a Tub*, a satire on 'corruptions in religion and learning'.
1701	Given prebend of St Patrick's, Dublin, as well as other livings. Wrote *Discourse of the Contests and Dissensions between the nobles and the commons in Athens and Rome*.

| 1708 | Published *Letter on the Sacramental Test*. |

Laws are like cobwebs, which may catch small flies, but let wasps and hornets break through.

A Critical Essay upon the Faculties of the Mind, 1709

1710	Attacked Whig ministers in the *Examiner*.
1711	Wrote *Conduct of the Allies*.
1713	Dean of St Patrick's, Dublin.

If Heaven had looked upon riches to be a valuable thing, it would not have given them to such a scoundrel.

Letter to Miss Vanhomrigh, 12–13 August 1720, *Correspondence of Jonathan Swift*, vol. 2, ed. H. Williams, 1963

| 1726 | Published *Gulliver's Travels*, for which he was paid £200. |

I cannot but conclude the bulk of your natives to be the most pernicious race of little odious vermin that nature ever suffered to crawl upon the surface of the earth.

Gulliver's Travels, 'A Voyage to Brobdingnag', ch. 6

And he gave it for his opinion, that whoever could make two ears of corn or two blades of grass to grow upon a spot of ground where only one grew before, would deserve better of mankind, and do more essential services to his country than the whole race of politicians put together.

Ibid., 'A Voyage to Brobdingnag', ch. 7

I told him . . . that we ate when we were not hungry, and drank without the provocation of thirst.

Ibid., 'A Voyage to the Houyhnhnms', ch. 6

| 1727 | Visited England.
Set up and paid for a monument to the Duke of Schomberg, Commander-in-Chief of William of Orange's forces at the Battle of the Boyne, in St Patrick's Cathedral. |

1727   Spent a third of his income on Charity and saved another
             third to found St Patrick's Hospital (opened 1757).

> So, naturalists observe, a flea
> Hath smaller fleas that on him prey;
> And these have smaller fleas to bite 'em,
> And so proceed ad infinitum.
> Thus every poet, in his kind,
> Is bit by him that comes behind.
>
> *On Poetry*, l. 337, 1733

1728   'Stella' died.

DEATH   1745 aged 77, having become paralysed and declared
             'unsound of mind'. Buried at St Patrick's Cathedral, Dublin.

HOBBIES & Ancient Greece and Rome.
INTERESTS

Sir Robert Walpole

English Whig statesman and first British Prime Minister,
who was also the first to occupy 10 Downing Street.
Saviour of the Establishment following the South Sea
Bubble débâcle which led to the ruin of many speculators.

BIRTH	1676, at Houghton, Norfolk. The fifth of 17 children, his father was the Whig MP for Castle Rising, Norfolk.
MARITAL STATUS	Married first, 1700, Catherine Shorter. Three daughters and two sons, including the historian Horace Walpole. Secondly, Maria Skerrit.
EDUCATION	Eton and King's College, Cambridge (Scholar).
CAREER	
1701–02	MP for Castle Rising, Norfolk.
1702–42	MP for King's Lynn.

A Little Bit of Background

William of Orange ousted James II in 1689, and reigned jointly with his wife, Mary, elder daughter of James, until her death in 1694, and then solely until his own death in 1702. Queen Anne, the second daughter of James II, reigned from 1702 to 1714. She also died childless, and was succeeded by George I, first monarch of the House of Hanover, 1714–27, who in turn was succeeded by George II, 1727–60.

1703	Leader of the Whig Party.
1708–10	Secretary at War.
1710–11	Treasurer of the Navy.
1711	Leader of the House of Commons.
1712	Expelled from the House of Commons and imprisoned in the Tower on a charge of corruption in the Navy Office.

Gratitude is a lively sense of future favours.

Lectures on the English Comic Writers, 'On Wit and Humour', William Hazlitt, 1819

1714	Privy Councillor.
1715–17	Prime Minister and Chancellor of the Exchequer.
1717	Thought up the first general sinking fund.
1720	Opposed the Government's encouragement of the South Sea Company. Yet supervised the speculation of Caroline, the Princess of Wales, in South Sea stock.
	Called upon to help the Government after the collapse of the South Sea Bubble.
1721–42	Prime Minister and Chancellor of the Exchequer.

All those men have their price.

Of fellow parliamentarians, *Memoirs of Sir Robert Walpole*, vol. 1, W. Coxe, 1798

1725	Knight of the Order of the Bath.
1726	Knight of the Order of the Garter.
1727	Reappointed First Lord of the Treasury and Chancellor of the Exchequer

'They now ring bells, but they will soon wring their hands.'

On the declaration of war with Spain, 1739, ibid., vol. 1

'Madam, there are fifty thousand men slain this year in Europe, and not one Englishman.'

To Queen Caroline, 1734, on the war of the Polish succession, in which the English had refused to participate, quoted in *Memoirs*, vol. 1, John Hervey, written 1734–43, published 1848

1742	Resigned all his affairs, pensioned and created Earl of Orford.
DEATH	1745, aged 69, in London. He died in debt and his grandson sold his art collection to Catherine the Great of Russia.
HOBBIES & INTERESTS	Investment and art.

Samuel Richardson

Industrious and successful printer who is credited with creating the modern novel. Clarissa, *which was published in seven volumes and consists of more than a million words, is the longest novel in the English language.*

BIRTH   1689, Mackworth, Derbyshire, the son of a joiner.

MARITAL STATUS   Married first, 1721, Martha Wilde, his master's daughter, d.1731. Six children, all of whom died in infancy. Secondly, 1733, Elizabeth Leake. Five daughters, four of whom survived, and one son, who died.

EDUCATION   'Common school learning'.

A Little Bit of Background

John Wesley founded the Methodist movement in 1729. William Hogarth produced *The Rake's Progress* in 1735. Handel's *Messiah* was first performed in 1742. Henry Fielding's, novel *Tom Jones* was published in 1749. Dr Johnson produced his *Dictionary* in 1755.

CAREER

1706	Apprenticed to a stationer.
	Became a printer in London.
1715	Became a Freeman of the Stationers' Company.
1721	Married Martha Wilde and set up business on his own.
1722	Took over printing of *The True Briton*.
1727	Appointed Renter Warden of the Stationers' Company.
1731	Wife died.
1733	Remarried.
1738	Published *The Apprentice's Vade Mecum*, on conduct and morals.
1739	Published his own version of *Aesop's Fables*.

1740	Published his first novel, in two volumes, *Pamela, or Virtue Rewarded*, in which the story is told through letters. The novel was quickly translated into French and Dutch.
1741	Published two further volumes of *Pamela*.
1742	Secured all the printing for the House of Commons.
1747	Published the first volumes of *Clarissa*, which became a European-wide success.

I have known a bird actually starve itself, and die with grief, at its being caught and caged — but never did I meet with a lady who was so silly . . . And yet we must all own that it is more difficult to catch a bird than a lady.

Clarissa, vol. 3, letter 75

1748	Published further volumes of *Clarissa*.
1750	Contributed to Dr Johnson's *Rambler*.
1753	Published *Sir Charles Grandison,* which met with equal success.
1754–5	Master of The Stationers' Company.

Instruction, Madam, is the pill; amusement is the gilding.

Letter to Lady Echlin, 22 September 1755

| **DEATH** | 1761, aged 72, in London. Buried in St Bride's Church, Fleet Street, London. |
| **HOBBIES & INTERESTS** | Illuminated manuscripts. |

John Wesley

English preacher and leader of the Methodist movement.

BIRTH	1703, at Epworth, Lincolnshire, son of the Rector of Epworth.
MARITAL STATUS	Married, 1751, Mary Vazeille, a widow. Separated 1776.
EDUCATION	1714, Foundationer at Charterhouse, London. Christ Church College, Oxford (Scholar).

 ## A Little Bit of Background

The Seven Years' War between France and England lasted from 1756 to 1763. The Bridgewater Canal, built to take coal from Worsley to Manchester, was completed in 1761. Colonial Stamp Duty was imposed in 1765. The Royal Crescent, Bath, was built between 1767 to 1776. James Watt built his steam engine in 1769. The Boston Tea Party took place in 1773. The War of American Independence lasted from 1775 to 1783.

CAREER

1725	Ordained deacon in the Anglican Church.
1726–51	Fellow of Lincoln College, Oxford.
1727–9	Curate for his father at Wroot.
1729–35	Tutor at Lincoln College, Oxford.
1729	Leader at the devotional group in Oxford started by his younger brother, Charles, dubbed 'methodists' on account of their methodical programme of study and prayer.
1733	Published prayers.
1735	Accepted leadership of Georgia mission in America.
1736	Founded a religious 'society' at Savannah, Georgia, based on the Moravian model, a Protestant group originally formed in Bohemia in 1457.
1737	Corresponded with Zinzendorf, the German bishop of the Moravian Brethren.

1737	Published first hymnal (to be followed by 22 further collections).
	Left Georgia to escape a libel action, based on his expulsion from communion of a woman who had rejected his offer of marriage and then accepted someone else's.
1738	Joined the Moravian Society.

> Thou hidden love of God, whose height,
> Whose depth unfathomed no man knows,
> I see from far thy beauteous light,
> Inly I sigh for thy repose.
>
> 'Divine Love' (a translation of G. Tersteegen's '*Verborgen Gottesliebe du*', 1729), in *A Collection of Psalms and Hymns*, 1738

Opened the first Methodist Chapel in Bristol.
And another in Moorfields, London.

> I went to America to convert the Indians; but oh, who shall convert me?
>
> *Journal*, 24 January 1738, ed. N. Curnock

> I felt my heart strangely warmed. I felt I did trust in Christ, Christ alone for salvation; and an assurance was given me that He had taken away my sins, even mine, and saved me from the law of sin and death.
>
> On his conversion, ibid., 24 May 1738

1739	Founded a 'united society' for weekday meetings – the official inception of Methodism.

> The Gospel of Christ knows of no religion but social; no holiness but social holiness.
>
> Preface, *Hymns and Sacred Poems*, 1739

> I look upon all the world as my parish.
>
> *Journal*, 11 June 1739, ed. N. Curnock

1740	Left the Moravian Society.
	Renounced Calvinism and published his 'free grace' sermon.
1741 & 44	Preached University sermons at Oxford.
1741	Introduced 'society tickets' of membership and divided the country into circuits.
1744	First Methodist Conversation (conference).
1745	Second Methodist Conversation acknowledged him as 'overseer'.

> I design plain truth for plain people.
>
> *Sermons on Several Occasions*, 1746

1747–90	Visited Isle of Man, Scotland and Ireland (42 times in total).
1751	Married Mary Vazeille.
1771–4	Published his *Works*.

> No circumstances can make it necessary for a man to burst in sunder all the ties of humanity.
>
> 'Thoughts upon Slavery', *Works* (Centenary ed.), vol. 11, 1774
>
> I let you loose, George, on the great continent of America. Publish your message in the open face of the sun, and do all the good you can.
>
> Letter to a preacher, George Shadford, March 1773, *Letters*, vol. 6, ed. J. Telford, 1931

1775–8	Wrote attacking agitation against taxes in the American colonies.
1776	Deserted by his wife.

> I have this day lived fourscore years . . . God grant that I may never live to be useless!
>
> *Journal*, 28 June 1783, ed. N. Curnock

1784	Produced his 'Deed of Declaration' (regulating chapels and preachers) and ordained presbyters to confer orders and administer sacraments.

Men may call me a knave or a fool, a rascal, a scoundrel, and I am content; but they shall never by my consent call me a Bishop!

Wesley Quotations, Betty M. Jarboe, 1990

DEATH	1791, aged 87, City Road, London. The house where he lived and died has been kept as a museum. Buried at the City Road Chapel, London.
HOBBIES & INTERESTS	Singing.

Henry Fielding

British novelist, dramatist and fighter for justice.
The author of the innovative Tom Jones, *he broke away*
from the epistolary method of novel writing used by his
contemporary Richardson.

BIRTH 1707, at Sharpham Park, near Glastonbury, Somerset, son of
General Edmund Fielding. His mother died when he was 11.

MARITAL Married first, 1734, Charlotte Cradock, d. 1744. One son and
STATUS one daughter, who died aged six. Secondly, Mary Daniel, his
first wife's former maid.

EDUCATION Sent to Eton when his father remarried, where he was a
contemporary and friend of William Pitt the Elder. Later
studied law at Leiden, Holland.

A Little Bit of Background

Pamela, by Samuel Richardson, was published in 1741.
Jonathan Swift published *Gulliver's Travels* in 1775. Dr Johnson's *Dictionary*
came out in 1755, the year of a catastrophic earthquake in Lisbon, Portugal.

CAREER
1726 Failed in his attempt to elope with an heiress.
1728–37 Wrote 25 dramas.
1734 Married Charlotte Cradock, the model for Sophia in *Tom Jones*.
1736–7 Opened a theatre in the Haymarket, London.
1737 The censorship introduced by the Licensing Act caused him
to abandon the theatre.
1740 Called to the Bar at Middle Temple.
1741 Published *An Apology for the Life of Mrs Shamela Andrews*,
a parody of Richardson's *Pamela*.

1742	Published *The History of the Adventures of Joseph Andrews and his friend, Mr Abraham Adams.*

I describe not men, but manners, not an individual, but a species.

Joseph Andrews, bk 3, ch. 1

Public schools are the nurseries of all vice and immorality.

Ibid., bk 3, ch. 5

1743	Published *Miscellanies*, which included *The Life and Death of Jonathan Wild the Great.*

He in a few minutes ravished this fair creature, or at least would have ravished her, if she had not, by a timely compliance, prevented him.

Jonathan Wild, bk 3, ch. 7, 1743

1744	Wife died.
1745–8	Issued weekly papers supporting the Government.
1748	JP for Westminster, where he fought embezzlement and corruption.
1749	Published *Tom Jones*, to huge public acclaim, though it was panned by Richardson, Tobias Smollett and Johnson.

When I mention religion, I mean the Christian religion; and not only the Christian religion, but the Protestant religion; and not only the Protestant religion but the Church of England.

Tom Jones, bk 3, ch. 3

What is commonly called love, namely the desire of satisfying a voracious appetite with a certain quantity of delicate white human flesh.

Ibid., bk 6, ch. 1

His designs were strictly honourable, as the phrase is; that is, to rob a lady of her fortune by way of marriage.

Ibid., bk 11, ch. 4

Henry Fielding

1750	Attacked gin drinking and public hanging.
1751	Published *Amelia*.

> It hath often been said, that it is not death, but dying, which is terrible.
>
> *Amelia*, bk 3, ch. 4
>
> One fool at least in every married couple.
>
> Ibid., bk 9, ch. 4

1753	Published 'A Proposal for Making Effective Provision for the Poor'.
1754	Travelled to Portugal to alleviate his gout and asthma. Wrote *Journal of a Voyage to Lisbon*, which was published after his death.
DEATH	1754, aged 47, in Lisbon, Portugal.
HOBBIES & INTERESTS	Theatre and justice.

William Pitt the Elder

British Whig statesman and Prime Minister, known as the Great Commoner, who was admired for his integrity and refusal to make money out of his high office. He opposed Sir Robert Walpole, supported the American colonists and encouraged an empire based on trade.

BIRTH   1708, in Westminster.

MARITAL   Married, 1754, Lady Hester Granville. Three sons, the second
STATUS   being William Pitt the Younger, and two daughters.

EDUCATION   Eton and Trinity College, Oxford.

 ## A Little Bit of Background

The War of the Austrian Succession lasted from 1740 to 1748. Bonnie Prince Charlie led the Jacobite Rebellion in 1745. The Seven Years' War, over the rival colonial ambitions of Britain and France, ended in 1763, Britain having gained India and Canada. The American Declaration of Independence was made in 1776.

CAREER
1731   Cornetcy in Lord Cobham's Horse.
1735   MP for Old Sarum (Salisbury), his first speech in the House
             of Commons causing his dismissal from the army.

> 'The atrocious crime of being a young man . . .
> I shall neither attempt to palliate nor deny.'
>
> Speech, House of Commons, 2 March 1741

1746   Joint Vice-Treasurer of Ireland.
             Paymaster General of the forces, where he refused to follow
             the usual practice of corruption.
1756–7   Prime Minister and Leader of the House of Commons.

1757–61	Prime Minister.

> 'The poorest man may in his cottage bid defiance to all the forces of the Crown. It may be frail – its roof may shake – the wind may blow through it – the storm may enter – the rain may enter – but the king of England cannot enter!'
>
> Speech, *c.* March 1763, quoted in *Historical Sketches of Statesmen in the Time of George III*, First Series, vol. 1, Lord Brougham, 1845

1766–8	Prime Minister.
1766	Created Earl of Chatham and Lord Privy Seal.
1771–4	Crippled by gout.

> 'You cannot conquer America.'
>
> Speech, House of Lords, 18 November 1777

DEATH	1778, aged 69. He was carried home to die after collapsing in the House of Commons. Buried in Westminster Abbey.
HOBBIES & INTERESTS	Backgammon.

Dr Johnson

Samuel Johnson, English poet, critic and lexicographer who produced the first English dictionary.

BIRTH	1709, Lichfield, Staffordshire, son of an elderly bookseller.
MARITAL STATUS	Married, 1735, 'Tetty' Porter, a widow 20 years his senior, d. 1752.
EDUCATION	Lichfield Grammar School and Pembroke College, Oxford, though he left after a year due to lack of money.

 ## A Little Bit of Background

Johnson was born in the reign of Queen Anne. Richardson's *Pamela* was published in 1741, Fielding's *Tom Jones* in 1749, Gibbon's *The Decline and Fall of the Roman Empire* and Adam Smith's *Wealth of Nations* in 1776. The year Captain Cook sighted Botany Bay, 1770, Gainsborough painted *The Blue Boy*.

CAREER **1737**	'Usher' (under-master) at Market Bosworth Grammar School. Went up to London with David Garrick, one of his pupils. Contributed to *The Gentleman's Magazine*.

> 'I'll come no more behind your scenes, David; for the silk stockings and white bosoms of your actresses excite my amorous propensities.'
>
> To Garrick; John Wilkes recalled the remark as being 'the silk stockings and white bosoms of your actresses do make my genitals to quiver'

1738	Published, anonymously, *London*, a long poem in the style of Alexander Pope.
1742	Employed in cataloguing the library of the Earl of Oxford.
1744	Published *Life of Mr Richard Savage*.
1747	Started work on his *Dictionary of the English Language*.

1749	Published the poem *The Vanity of Human Wishes.*
	Produced the play *Irene* at Drury Lane.
1750	Started *The Rambler*, a periodical written almost entirely by himself.

I have laboured to refine our language to grammatical purity, and to clear it from colloquial barbarisms, licentious idioms, and irregular combinations.

In the *Rambler*, no. 208, 14 March 1752

1752	Widowed.

'They teach the morals of a whore, and the manners of a dancing master.'

On *Letters to his Son*, Lord Chesterfield, a volume containing advice on behaviour in polite society, quoted in *Life of Samuel Johnson*, James Boswell, 1791, 1754

1755	His *Dictionary* published. Rebuffed Lord Chesterfield's belated offer of patronage.

But these were the dreams of a poet doomed at last to wake a lexicographer.

Preface, *Dictionary of the English Language*

Dull. To make dictionaries is dull work.

Ibid., eighth definition of the word 'dull'

Lexicographer. A writer of dictionaries, a harmless drudge.

Ibid.

Patron. Commonly a wretch who supports with insolence, and is paid with flattery.

Ibid.

'If a madman were to come into this room with a stick in his hand, no doubt we should pity the state of his mind; but our primary consideration would be to take care of ourselves. We should knock him down first and pity him afterwards.'

Life of Samuel Johnson, James Boswell, 1791.

'Ignorance, madam, pure ignorance.'

On being asked why he had defined pastern as the 'knee' of a horse, ibid.

1756	Arrested for debt (bailed by the author, Samuel Richardson).
1756–8	Contributed to the *Literary Magazine*.

The only end of writing is to enable the readers better to enjoy life, or better to endure it.

A Free Enquiry, 1757, ed. D. Greene, 1984

1758–60	Wrote the *Idler* for the *Universal Chronicle*.

'Difficult do you call it Sir? I wish it were impossible.'

On the performance of a celebrated violinist,
Anecdotes of Distinguished Persons, Supplement, William Seward, 1797.

'Was there ever yet anything written by mere man that was wished longer by its readers, excepting *Don Quixote*, *Robinson Crusoe*, and *The Pilgrim's Progress?*'

Anecdotes of . . . Johnson, Hester Lynch Piozzi, 1786

'I have always said, the first Whig was the Devil.'

Life of Samuel Johnson, James Boswell, 1791

When two Englishmen meet, their first talk is of the weather.

Idler, no. 11, 24 June 1758

Among the calamities of war may be jointly numbered the diminution of the love of truth, by the falsehoods which interest dictates and credulity encourages.

Ibid., no. 30, 11 November 1758

1759	Wrote the philosophical fable *Rasselas, Prince of Abyssinia*.

Liberty is, to the lowest rank of every nation, little more than the choice of working or starving.

'The Bravery of the English Common Soldier', *The British Magazine*, January 1760

1762	Granted a pension of £300 per annum by Lord Bute.
1760–5	Wrote pamphlets.
1763	Met James Boswell and founded his Literary Club.

'The noblest prospect which a Scotchman ever sees, is the high road that leads him to England!'

6 July 1763, *Life of Samuel Johnson*, James Boswell, 1791

'A woman's preaching is like a dog's walking on his hinder legs. It is not done well; but you are surprised to find it done at all.'

31 July 1763, ibid.

1765	Finished his edition of Shakespeare.
1767	Met George III.

'The triumph of hope over experience.'

Of a man who remarried immediately after the death of a wife with whom he had been unhappy, ibid.

1773	Travelled in Scotland with Boswell.

'Read over your compositions, and where ever you meet with a passage which you think is particularly fine, strike it out.'

Quoting a college tutor, 30 April 1773, ibid.

'I have, all my life long, been lying till noon; yet I tell all young men, and tell them with great sincerity, that nobody who does not rise early will ever do any good.'

14 September 1773, *Tour to the Hebrides*, James Boswell, 1785

1774	Went to Wales with his friends the Thrales.
1775	Went to Paris with the Thrales.
	Published *Journey to the Western Isles of Scotland.*

'There are few ways in which a man can be more innocently employed than in getting money.'

27 March 1775, *Life of Samuel Johnson*, James Boswell, 1791

'We would all be idle if we could.'

1776, ibid.

'Sir, you have but two topics, yourself and me. I am sick of both.'

May 1776, ibid.

'If I had no duties, and no reference to futurity, I would spend my life in driving briskly in a postchaise with a pretty woman.'

19 September 1777, ibid.

'When a man is tired of London, he is tired of life.'

20 September 1777, ibid.

1779 & **81**   Published *Lives of the Poets* (for which he 'named his own price').

'Sir, I have two very cogent reasons for not printing any list of subscribers; – one, that I have lost all the names, – the other, that I have spent all the money.'

May 1781, ibid.

'I hate a fellow whom pride, or cowardice, or laziness drives into a corner, and who does nothing when he is there but sit and growl; let him come out as I do, and bark.'

Of Jeremiah Markland, 10 October 1782, ibid.

Resolve not to be poor: whatever you have, spend less. Poverty is a great enemy to human happiness; it certainly destroys liberty, and it makes some virtues impracticable, and others extremely difficult.

Letter to Boswell, 7 December 1782, ibid.

The black dog I hope always to resist, and in time to drive, though I am deprived of almost all those that used to help me . . . when I rise my breakfast is solitary, the black dog waits to share it, from breakfast to dinner he continues barking, except that Dr. Brocklesby for a little keeps him at a distance . . . Night comes at last, and some hours of restlessness and confusion bring me again to a day of solitude. What shall exclude the black dog from a habitation like this?

On his attacks of melancholia; letter to Mrs Thrale, 28 June 1783,
Letters of Samuel Johnson, ed. R.W. Chapman, vol. 3, 1952

'It is as bad as bad can be: it is ill-fed, ill-killed, ill-kept, and ill-drest.'

On the roast mutton he had been served at an inn, 3 June 1784,
Life of Samuel Johnson, James Boswell, 1791

Dictionaries are like watches, the worst is better than none, and the best cannot be expected to go quite true.

Letter to Francesco Sastres, 21 August 1784, ibid.

DEATH	1784, aged 75. Buried in Westminster Abbey.
HOBBIES & INTERESTS	Poetry and clubs.

Bonnie Prince Charlie

Charles Edward Louis Philip Casimir Stuart, the Young Pretender.

BIRTH 1720, Rome, eldest son of the eldest son of James II.

MARITAL STATUS Married, 1772, Louisa von Stolberg, separated 1780. One illegitimate daughter, Charlotte, by his mistress Clementina Walkinshaw.

EDUCATION In Rome.

CAREER

1734 Served at Gaeta.

1744 Head of French invasion foiled by the English Fleet at Dunkirk.

1745 Landed in the Hebrides.
Raised his standard at Glenfinnan.
Entered Edinburgh.
Victorious at Preston Pans.
Reached Carlisle and Derby, prompting the fourth verse of The National Anthem (now no longer sung):

> God grant that Marshal Wade,
> May by thy mighty aid,
> Victory bring.
> May he sedition hush,
> And like a torrent rush,
> Rebellious Scots to crush
> God save the King!

1746 Victorious at Falkirk.
Overwhelmingly defeated at Culloden.
Fled to the Highlands with a £30,000 price on his head, but no one betrayed him. Escaped to France, aided by Flora Macdonald.

A Little Bit of Background

Bonnie Prince Charlie's Catholic grandfather was ousted by William and Mary in 1688. The Act of Settlement in 1701 bars Catholics from the throne. 1707 saw the Union of England and Scotland. The first Jacobite Rebellion of 1715 rose in support of Bonnie Prince Charlie's father, James, the Old Pretender. The Scottish Jacobites were defeated at Sheriffmuir and the English Jacobites at Preston.

1748	Expelled from France. His supporters disillusioned by his drunkenness and his loyalty to his mistress, Clementina Walkinshaw, who was an English spy.
1750/2/4	Visited London.
1754	Lived in Basle.
1766	Titular King.
1772	Pensioned by France.
	Married.
1780	Separated from his wife and moved to Florence.
DEATH	1788, aged 67, in Rome, after 40 years wandering Europe.
HOBBIES & INTERESTS	Gambling and drink.

Adam Smith

Scottish political philosopher and economist,
author of the Wealth of Nations, *which revolutionised*
economic theory.

BIRTH	1723, at Kirkcaldy, Fife, posthumous son of a comptroller of customs.
MARITAL STATUS	Single.
EDUCATION	Glasgow University and Balliol College, Oxford (Snell Exhibitioner).

 ## A Little Bit of Background

Having been bankrupted by the colonisation of Darien fiasco, Scotland was united with England in 1707. The Bridgewater Canal, built to take coal from Worsley to Manchester, was completed in 1761. The Spinning Jenny was invented in 1764.

CAREER

1751	Elected to Chair of Logic at Glasgow University.
1752	Transferred to Chair of Moral Philosophy at Glasgow University.
1759	Published *Theory of the Moral Sentiments*.
1762	Appointed Vice Rector of Glasgow University.
	Became tutor to the Duke of Buccleuch. Visited Paris and Geneva.
1766	Stayed in London.
1767	Settled in Kirkcaldy on a pension from the Duke of Buccleuch.
1776	Published *Inquiry into the nature and causes of the Wealth of Nations*.

It is not from the benevolence of the butcher, the brewer, or the baker, that we expect our dinner, but from their regard to their own interest. We address ourselves not to their humanity but their self love.

Wealth of Nations, bk 1, ch. 2

People of the same trade seldom meet together, even for merriment and diversion, but the conversation ends in a conspiracy against the public, or in some contrivance to raise prices.

Ibid., bk 1, ch. 10, pt 2

To found a great empire for the sole purpose of raising up a people of customers, may at first sight appear a project fit only for a nation of shopkeepers. It is, however, a project altogether unfit for a nation of shopkeepers; but extremely fit for a nation whose government is influenced by shopkeepers.

Ibid., bk 4, ch. 7, pt 3

Consumption is the sole end purpose of production; and the interest of the producer ought to be attended to only so far as it may be necessary for promoting that of the consumer.

Ibid., bk 4, ch. 8

There is no art which one government sooner learns of another than that of draining money from the pockets of the people.

Ibid., bk 5, ch. 2

> If any of the provinces of the British empire cannot be made to contribute towards the support of the whole empire, it is surely time that Great Britain should free herself from the expense of defending those provinces in time of war, and of supporting any part of their civil or military establishments in time of peace, and endeavour to accommodate her future views and designs to the real mediocrity of her circumstances.
>
> Ibid., bk 5, ch. 3

1778 Elected Lord Rector of Glasgow University.

DEATH 1790, aged 67, in Edinburgh. Buried in Canongate Kirkyard, Edinburgh.

HOBBIES & INTERESTS A member of Dr Johnson's Literary Club.

Clive of India

Robert Clive, British general, victor at Plassey and first Governor of Bengal.

BIRTH	1725, Styche, Market Drayton, son of a lawyer, the eldest of 13 children. He was brought up by his uncle near Eccles.
MARITAL STATUS	Married, 1753, Margaret Maskelyne, sister of the astronomer royal. One son, Edward, who later became Governor of Madras.
EDUCATION	Market Drayton School, where he ran a protection racket extorting money from shopkeepers in return for not breaking their windows, and Merchant Taylors' School.

A Little Bit of Background

The East India Company was founded in 1600 and set up a trading base in Surat on the west coast of India. Charles II's Portuguese wife, Catherine of Braganza, brought Bombay with her as part of her dowry. Like the Portuguese and French, who were also trading in India, the British were forced to take sides in local politics or abandon their investments. Eventually, the French and English East India companies had their own armies. Britain continued to increase its influence in India after Plassey, but 100 years later, the sepoys rose in revolt in the Indian Mutiny. After monstrous violence on both sides, Britain restored order and the Government took over from the East India company completely.

CAREER	
1743	Clerk in East India Company.
1744	Arrived in Madras, having spent all his money and incurred debts on the difficult and unusually long voyage.
1745	Twice attempted to blow his brains out; each time the pistol misfired.

> 'I feel that I am reserved for some end or other.'
>
> After his pistol twice failed to fire, while attempting to take his own life,
> *The Life of Robert, First Lord Clive*, G.R. Gleig, ch. 1, 1848

1746	Captured by the French. Escaped to Fort David.
1747	Ensign in the Army of the East India Company.
1748	His conspicuous gallantry remarked on at the siege of Pondicherry.
1749	Lieutenant.
1750	Captain.
1751	Captured Arcot. Commanded a force of 80 British soldiers and 150 sepoys that repulsed attacks by a force of 10,000.
	Won at Avri.
	Took Conjeveram twice.
	Defeated the French at Caveripak.
	Involved in the capture of Trichinopoly.
	Took Covelong and Chingleput.
1753	Invalided to England, where he paid off his father's debts.
1755	Sent back to Bombay as Lieutenant Colonel.
1756	Defeated the pirate Angria at Gheviah.
	Assumed command at Fort St David.
	Retook Calcutta after the Nawab of Bengal had attacked the British garrison and imprisoned 146 men in a cellar, the 'Black Hole of Calcutta', 123 of whom died.
	Took Chandernagore.
1757	Defeated the Nawab of Bengal's army of 68,000 at the Battle of Plassey with a force of only 3,000 men. Accepted a massive 'present' from the new Nawab he installed.
1757–60	Governor of Bengal.
1759	Thwarted the Dutch at Chinseura.
1760–74	Returned to England and became MP for Shrewsbury.
1762	Made Baron Clive (Irish peer).
1765	Returned to Bengal, rectified abuses and founded a pension fund for disabled officers.
1766	Returned to England in poor health.

1772–3	The subject of a Parliamentary inquiry. He defended himself before his peers in an all-night sitting in the House of Lords.

'A great prince was dependent on my pleasure, an opulent city lay at my mercy; its richest bankers bid against each other for my smiles; I walked through vaults which were thrown open to me alone, piled on either hand with gold and jewels!

By God, Mr Chairman, at this moment I stand astonished at my own moderation!'

Reply during Parliamentary cross-examination, 1773, ibid., ch. 29

DEATH	1774, aged 49, from suicide, as a result of depression, probably exacerbated by an addiction to opium, in Berkeley Square, London. Buried in St Margaret's Churchyard, Moreton Say, Leicestershire.
HOBBIES & INTERESTS	Opium.

Thomas Gainsborough

English portrait and landscape painter who created a
stunning record of Georgian life.

BIRTH	1727, Sudbury, Suffolk.
MARITAL STATUS	Married, 1746, Margaret Burr. Two daughters.
EDUCATION	Taught by Gravelot and Hayman in London.

A Little Bit of Background

Hogarth's *The Rake's Progress* was painted in 1735. Sir Joshua Reynolds became the first President of the Royal Academy in 1768. The Royal Crescent, Bath, was completed in 1776.

CAREER

1746–60   Moved to Ipswich, where he painted portraits, including *Mr and Mrs Andrews* (1748).

1760–74   Lived in Bath (20 of his pictures being exhibited by the Society of Artists), where he painted *The Harvest Wagon*.

> Damn gentlemen. There is not such a set of enemies to a real artist in the world as they are, if not kept at a proper distance.
>
> Letter to the musician William Jackson, 2 September 1767,
> *The Letters of Thomas Gainsborough*, ed. Mary Woodall, 1961

1768   Founding member of the Royal Academy.

> 'Recollect that painting and punctuality mix like oil and vinegar, and that genius and regularity are utter enemies, and must be to the end of time.'
>
> Speech to Edward Stratford, 1 May 1772, ibid.

1774	Moved to London, where he painted portraits of *The Blue Boy* and the *Duchess of Devonshire*, and landscapes.
1784	Withdrew all his work and refused to hang his pictures at the Royal Academy following a row about the hanging of a painting. From then on, he exhibited in his own house.
DEATH	1788, aged 61, of cancer. Buried at St Anne's, Kew Green, Richmond.
HOBBIES & INTERESTS	Fishing.

General Wolfe

James Wolfe's capture of Quebec led France to cede Canada to Britain at the end of the Seven Years' War.

BIRTH | 1727, Westerham, Kent, eldest son of General Edward Wolfe.

MARITAL STATUS | Single.

EDUCATION | Joined the Marines at the age of 14.

 A Little Bit of Background

The Seven Years' War began in 1756. By the time it ended, the British had taken Quebec and Guadeloupe, expelled the French from India, defeated them at the Battle of Minden and sank the French Fleet at Quiberon Bay.

CAREER

1741	Second Lieutenant of Marines.
1742	Ensign.
1743	In Flanders.
1743	Lieutenant. Acting Adjutant at Dettingen.
1744	Served with Marshal Wade.
1745	Brigade Major at Falkirk.
	On staff at Culloden.
1747	In Holland.
1749	Major 20th Foot.
1750	Lieutenant Colonel.
1749–52	In Scotland.
1752–3	Studying in Paris.
1753	In Scotland.
1754–5	At Exeter.
1755–6	At Canterbury, where he revised and improved manoeuvres.
1757–8	Quartermaster-General in Ireland.

1758	At Rochefort.
	Brigadier in siege at Louisbourg.
	Colonel 67th Regiment.
	Returned to England
1759	Major General at Quebec.

The General . . . repeated nearly the whole of Gray's Elegy . . . adding, as he concluded, that he would prefer being the author of that poem to the glory of beating the French tomorrow.

Biographical Account of J. Robinson in Transactions of the Royal Society of Edinburgh,
vol. 7, J. Playfair, 1815

DEATH	1759, aged 32, having scaled the heights above Quebec, he was shot on the Plains of Abraham, and died having learnt of his victory. Buried in St Alphege's, Greenwich, London.

'Now God be praised I will die in peace.'

Last words

HOBBIES & INTERESTS	Poetry.

Captain James Cook

Circumnavigator of the globe, who explored the Pacific and claimed Botany Bay for Britain. His use of lime juice to prevent scurvy earned British sailors the nickname 'limeys'.

BIRTH	1728, Marton, North Yorkshire, son of an agricultural labourer.
MARITAL STATUS	Married, 1762, Elizabeth Batts. Six children, all of whom died young.
EDUCATION	At sea.

 ## A Little Bit of Background

After America won her independence in 1776, Britain had to look elsewhere for a place to send her convicts – the first consignment reached Botany Bay in 1788.

CAREER	Merchant seaman in the Baltic trade.
1755	Seaman in the Royal Navy.
1759	Master in the Royal Navy.
	Surveyed the St Lawrence River, Canada.
1759–67	On the North American Station.
1766–8	Published *Sailing Directions*.
1768	Lieutenant in the Royal Navy.
	Set sail in HMS *Endeavour* for Tahiti to observe the transit of Venus and then to search for a continent thought to exist in the south central Pacific.
1769–70	Mapped the coast of New Zealand, the east coast of Australia and part of New Guinea.
1771	Returned to England via the Cape of Good Hope.
1771	Commander.
1772	Set sail in the *Resolution* to verify the existence of an Antarctic continent.

| 1773–5 | Touched on Pacific Islands and the Antarctic ice fields. |

I, who had ambition not only to go farther than any one had gone before, but as far as it was possible for man to go, was not sorry at meeting with this interruption as it in some measure relieved us, at least shortened the dangers and hardships inseparable with the navigation of the Southern Polar Regions. Since therefore, we could not proceed one inch farther to the south, no other reason need be assigned for my tacking and standing back to the north.

Extract from the journal of Captain James Cook,
describing meeting ice on his journey to Antarctica, 1774

1775	His prevention of scurvy through the use of lime juice adopted by the Royal Navy.
1775	Captain.
1776	Tried to sail round North America from the Pacific.
1778	Discovered the Sandwich Islands.
	Mapped the Pacific coast of North America.
DEATH	1779, aged 50, clubbed and stabbed in Hawaii, attempting to refit after a storm. Buried in the waters of Kealakekua Bay, Hawaii.
HOBBIES & INTERESTS	Herbal medicine.

Edmund Burke

*Irish-born British politician and philosopher whose
championship of a just relationship between rulers and the
ruled led him to condemn the French revolutionaries but
sympathise with the American.*

BIRTH	1729, Dublin, Ireland.
MARITAL STATUS	Married, 1757, Jane Nugent. Two sons, Richard and Christopher.
EDUCATION	Trinity College, Dublin.

 ## A Little Bit of Background

The War of American Independence lasted from 1775 to 1783.
George Washington became the first President of the United States in
1789, the year of the Storming of the Bastille in Paris.

CAREER

1750	Entered Middle Temple, London.
1755	His allowance from his father withdrawn for 'idleness'.
1756	Published *Vindication of Natural Society* and *On the Sublime and Beautiful*.
	Married his doctor's daughter, who abandoned her Catholic faith to join him as a Protestant.
1759	Founded the *Annual Register*.
1759–64	Secretary to William Gerard Hamilton.
1761–4	Accompanied Hamilton to Ireland.
1764	Relinquished the pension Hamilton secured for him.
1765	Secretary to the Marquis of Rockingham.
	Inherited a modest estate in Ireland.
1765–74	MP for Wendover, Buckinghamshire.
1768	Bought an estate at Beaconsfield, Buckinghamshire.
1769	Financial problems.

| 1770 | Published *Thoughts on the Cause of the Present Discontents.* |

> When bad men combine, the good must associate; else they will fall, one by one, an unpitied sacrifice in a contemptible struggle.
>
> *Thoughts on the Cause of the Present Discontents*

1771	Won campaign to publicise proceedings in Parliament. Agent for New York Province.
1773	Visited Paris.
1774–80	MP for Bristol.

> 'Your representative owes you, not his industry only, but his judgement; and he betrays, instead of serving you, if he sacrifices it to your opinion.'
>
> Speech, 3 November 1774, *Speeches at his Arrival at Bristol*

| 1775–6 | Proposed Peace with America. |

> The concessions of the weak are the concessions of fear.
>
> *On Conciliation with America*, 1775

1780	Attacked the slave trade.
1781–94	MP for Malton.
1782	Paymaster of the Forces. Retired from Ministry.
1783	Paymaster of Forces.
1784/5	Lord Rector of Glasgow University.
1785	Travelled in Scotland.
1785–95	Involved in the impeachment of Warren Hastings, first Governor General of India, who was accused of corruption but acquitted on all charges.
1788–9	Backed William Wilberforce's campaign for the abolition of the slave trade.
1790	Condemned French democracy in Parliament. Published *Reflections on the French Revolution.*

A state without the means of some change is without the means of its conservation.

Reflections on the Revolution in France

People will not look forward to posterity, who never look backward to their ancestors.

Ibid.

Whatever each man can separately do, without trespassing upon others, he has a right to do for himself; and he has a right to a fair portion of all which society, with all its combinations of skills and force, can do in his favour.

Ibid.

I thought ten thousand swords must have leapt from their scabbards to avenge even a look that threatened her with insult.

Of Marie Antoinette, ibid.

1794	Retired from Parliament.
1795	Involved in the founding of Maynooth College.
1796	Established a school for the sons of French refugees. Wrote *Letters on a Regicide Peace*.

It is necessary only for the good man to do nothing for evil to triumph.

DEATH	1797, aged 68, at Beaconsfield Church, Buckinghamshire.
HOBBIES & INTERESTS	Freedom.

King George III

King of Great Britain and Ireland from 1760 to 1820,
who was blamed for the loss of the American colonies, but
became a symbol of patriotic pride during the wars with
the French.

BIRTH	1738, prematurely, at Norfolk House, London, eldest son of Frederick Louis, Prince of Wales, who died after being struck on the head with a cricket ball.
MARITAL STATUS	Married, 1761, Charlotte Sophia of Mecklenburg-Strelitz. Nine sons, including the future kings George IV and William IV. Six daughters.

A Little Bit of Background

The loss of the American colonies was finalised at the Treaty of Versailles in 1783. France rose in revolt in 1789 and was almost continuously at war with Britain from 1793 to 1815.

EDUCATION	In England.
CAREER	
1751	Created Prince of Wales on the death of his father.
1760	Crowned on the death of his grandfather.

> 'Born and educated in this country, I glory in the name of Briton.'
>
> The King's speech on Opening the Session, House of Lords, 18 November 1760

1761	Married Charlotte Sophia of Mecklenburg-Strelitz.
1765	First attack of madness.
1770	Personally directed government for the next 12 years.
1775	Approved every means of distressing America.

> 'Balderdash!'
>
> Reaction on having been read the American Declaration
> of Independence, 1776

1780 Regarded as having saved London through his conduct
during the Gordon Riots, a week of public disorder during
which property was destroyed and 300 people died.

> 'Was there ever such stuff as the great part of Shakespeare? Only
> one must not say so! But what think you? — What? — Is there not
> sad stuff? — What? — What?'
>
> To the novelist Fanny Burney, 19 December 1785,
> quoted in *Diary and Letters of Madame d'Arblay*, vol. 2, 1842

1788–9 Second serious attack of madness.
1800 Shot at by an assassin.
1803 Third attack of madness – assumed then to have been
caused by distress at the thought of Catholic emancipation.
1804 Fourth attack of madness – assumed then to have been
caused by the conduct of the Prince of Wales.
1811 Blind and mad, his son, the future George IV, appointed
Regent.

DEATH 1820, aged 81. Buried at St George's Chapel, Windsor.

HOBBIES & Farming and craftsmanship.
INTERESTS

William Blake

Romantic non-conformist poet and painter, author of Jerusalem.

BIRTH	1757, Golden Square, London, third son of a hosier.
MARITAL STATUS	Married, 1782, Catherine Boucher.
EDUCATION	1767, Pars Drawing School, The Strand, where he started writing original verse, some of which was published in poetical sketches. 1771, apprentice to James Basire, engraver to the Society of Antiquities, where he was set the task of drawing the monuments of the old churches of London. 1778, student at the Royal Academy.

A Little Bit of Background

George III reigned from 1760 to 1820, a period of industrialisation at home and war overseas. Sir Joshua Reynolds became the first President of the Royal Academy in 1768. Coleridge and Wordsworth published their joint collection of poetry, *Lyrical Ballads*, in 1798.

CAREER

1779	Bookseller's engraver.
1784	Opened a print shop in partnership with his brother.
1787	On the death of his brother, he closed the shop and, using his last half crown, published his *Songs of Innocence* as an 'illuminated book', the method revealed to him in a dream by his dead brother.
1791	Wrote *Songs of Experience* and was employed by a bookseller to illustrate children's stories.
1793	Moved to Lambeth, where he continued writing and illustrating.

Exuberance is beauty.

The Marriage of Heaven and Hell, 'Proverbs of Hell'

Energy is Eternal Delight.

Ibid., 'The Voice of the Dead'

Prisons are built with stones of Law, brothels
with bricks of religion.

Ibid., 'Proverbs of Hell'

Tyger Tyger, burning bright,
In the forest of the night;
What immortal hand or eye,
Could frame thy fearful symmetry?

Songs of Experience, 'The Tyger', 1791

1800 The sculptor Flaxman introduced him to an admiring squire
who set him up in a cottage by the sea. After three years,
he moved back to London in order to 'be no longer
pestered with the squire's gentle ignorance and polite
disapprobation'.

1803 Charged with sedition by a drunken sailor, provoked in part
by his habit of wearing the red bonnet of the Jacobins, and
acquitted.

To see a world in a grain of sand
And a heaven in a wild flower,
Hold infinity in the palm of your hand
And eternity in an hour.

'Auguries of Innocence', 1803

A robin red breast in a cage
Puts all Heaven in a rage.

Ibid.

1808 Exhibited in the Royal Academy for the last time.

What it will be questioned when the sun rises do you not see a round disc of fire somewhat like a guinea O no no I see an innumerable company of the heavenly host crying Holy, Holy, Holy is the Lord God Almighty.

Descriptive Catalogue, 'The Vision of Judgement' 1810

1818	Met John Linnell, a young artist who supported him for the rest of his life.
DEATH	1827, aged 69. Buried in Bunhill Fields Burial Ground, City Road, London.
HOBBIES & INTERESTS	Flower arranging.

Lord Nelson

Horatio Nelson, British admiral and victor at Trafalgar,
worshipped by the British public for his dash and success,
despite a scandalous affair with Lady Hamilton.

BIRTH 1758, Burnham Thorpe Rectory, Norfolk.

MARITAL Married, 1787, Frances Nisbet, a widow. Separated 1800.
STATUS One illegitimate daughter, Horatia, the result of his affair
with Emma, Lady Hamilton.

EDUCATION At sea.

 A Little Bit of Background

Britain was at war with Revolutionary France from 1793 to
1802 and again from 1803 to 1815.

CAREER

1770	Joined the Navy. Served in the West Indies.
1778	Made Commander.
1779	Made Captain.
1780	Returned to England due to ill health.
1782	Took a convoy to America and returned to the West Indies.
1783	On half-pay.
1784	Learnt French at St Omer and appointed to the ship HMS *Boreas*
1787	Married Mrs Nisbet.
1787–93	Unemployed.
1793	Sailed to the Mediterranean and met Sir William and Lady Hamilton in Naples.
1794	Lost the sight of his right eye when attacking Calvi in Corsica.
1796	Commodore.

| 1797 | Involved in the Battle of Cape St Vincent and made KB and Rear-Admiral. |

> You must consider every man your enemy who speaks ill of your king; and . . . you must hate a Frenchman as you hate the devil.
>
> *Life of Nelson*, Robert Southey, ch. 1, 1813

| 1797 | Failed to take a Spanish treasure ship at Santa Cruz, Tenerife, where his right arm was shattered. |
| 1798 | Sought out the French Fleet in Aboukir Bay, the Nile, and destroyed it. |

> 'Before this time tomorrow I shall have gained a peerage, or Westminster Abbey.'
>
> Comments before the Battle of the Nile, 1798, ibid., ch. 5

1798	Created Baron Nelson of the Nile.
	Went to Naples.
1799	Restored order in Naples and made Duke of Bronté.
1800	Returned home with the Hamiltons, due to ill health.
	Separated from his wife.
1801	Commanded attack on Copenhagen. Made Viscount Nelson.

> 'I have only one eye – I have a right to be blind sometimes . . . I really do not see the signal.'
>
> On putting his telescope to his blind eye and ignoring a signal from his commander-in-chief, Sir Hyde Parker, ordering a retreat at the Battle of Copenhagen, 1801, *Life of Nelson*, Robert Southey, ch. 7, 1813

1801–3	Shared a house with the Hamiltons.
1803–5	Appointed to the Mediterranean, watching the French Fleet at Toulon.
1805	Defeated the combined French and Spanish fleets at Trafalgar.

'In honour I gained them, and in honour I will die with them.'

When asked to cover the stars on his uniform, ibid., ch. 9

May the Great God, whom I worship, grant to my Country and for the benefit of Europe in general a great and glorious victory; and may no misconduct in anyone tarnish it; and may humanity after Victory be the predominant feature of the British Fleet. For myself, individually, I commit my life to Him who made me, and may His blessing light upon my endeavours for serving my Country faithfully. To Him I resign myself and the just cause which is entrusted to me to defend. Amen. Amen. Amen.

Diary entry on the eve of the Battle of Trafalgar, 21 October 1805, *Dispatches and Letters of Nelson*, Nicholas Harris Nicolas, vol. 7, 1846

England expects that every man will do his duty.

At the Battle of Trafalgar, 21 October 1805, *Life of Nelson*, Robert Southey, ch. 9, 1813

'Kiss me, Hardy.'

As he lay dying at the Battle of Trafalgar, 21 October 1805, ibid.

DEATH 1805, aged 47. Killed at the Battle of Trafalgar by a musket shot on the quarter deck of his flag ship, HMS *Victory*. His body was brought back to England preserved in a casket of French brandy and lay in state at Greenwich before being buried in St Paul's Cathedral. A brandy-based drink was created in memory of this, called Nelson's Blood.

HOBBIES & INTERESTS Lady Hamilton and glory.

William Pitt the Younger

British Tory Prime Minister, 1783–1801 and 1804–6, who first came to office at the astonishingly young age of 24, and who guided Europe through the Napoleonic wars with France. Faced with the task of restoring the country's finances after the expense of the War of American Independence, he was responsible for introducing income tax.

BIRTH
1759, Hayes, Kent, second son of William Pitt the Elder.

MARITAL STATUS
Single.

EDUCATION
A sickly child, he was educated at home until he went up to Pembroke College, Cambridge, at the age of 14.

CAREER

1780 Called to the Bar at Lincoln's Inn.
1781 MP for Appleby.
1782 Chancellor of the Exchequer.
1783 Prime Minister.

> 'Necessity is the plea for every infringement of human freedom: it is the argument of tyrants; it is the creed of slaves.'
>
> Speech, House of Commons, 18 November 1783

1786 Instituted the sinking fund for paying off the National Debt.
1793 Declared war against France (at war until 1802).
Suspended the Habeas Corpus Act.

> We must anew commence the salvation of Europe.
>
> 1795, quoted in *Dictionary of National Biography*, 1917

1798 Introduced income tax.
1800 United the Irish Parliament with that of Great Britain.

| 1801 | Resigned as Prime Minister. |

'We must recollect . . . what it is we have at stake, what it is we have to contend for. It is for our property, it is for our liberty, it is for our independence, nay, for our existence as a nation; it is for our character, it is for our very name as Englishmen, it is for everything dear and valuable to man on this side of the grave.'

> Speech on once more being at war with France, 22 July 1803,
> *Speeches of Rt. Hon. William Pitt*, vol. 4, 1806

'England has saved herself by her exertions, and will, as I trust, save Europe by her example.'

> Replying to a toast in which he had been described as the saviour of his country
> in the wars with France, *War Speeches of William Pitt*, R. Coupland, 1915

| 1804 | Prime Minister. |

'Roll up that map; it will not be wanted these ten years.'

> Of a map of Europe, on hearing of Napoleon's victory
> at Austerlitz, December 1805, *Life of the Rt. Hon. William Pitt*,
> *Earl Stanhope*, vol. 4, ch. 43, 1862

'Oh, my country! How I leave my country!'

> Reputed last words

'I think I could eat one of Bellamy's veal pies.'

> Alternative last words; Bellamy was the first person to run
> a refreshment room in the House of Commons

| **DEATH** | 1806, aged 46, after several years of ill health, in London. |
| **HOBBIES &** **INTERESTS** | Government. |

William Wilberforce

Politician and devout Christian who was the driving force behind the movement to abolish slavery.

BIRTH	1759, Hull.
MARITAL STATUS	Married, 1825, Barbara Ann Spooner. Four sons, William, Robert, Samuel and Henry, and two daughters who predeceased him.
EDUCATION	St John's College, Cambridge.

 ## A Little Bit of Background

In 1772, the Lord Chief Justice, Lord Mansfield, decreed that slavery was illegal in England, thus freeing all the slaves in England, but not overseas. The slave *trade* was abolished by Wilberforce's bill in 1807; *slavery* itself was not abolished in the whole of the British Empire until 1833.

CAREER	
1780	MP for Hull.
1784	MP for Yorkshire.
1784–5	In Europe. Became a religious 'enthusiast'.
1786	His bill amending criminal law was rejected by the House of Lords.
1787	Founded the 'Proclamation Society' (for the suppression of vice).
	Led movement in Parliament to abolish slavery.

> God Almighty has set me two great objects, the suppression of the Slave Trade and the reformation of manners.
>
> Diary, 1787

1791	His motion for the abolition of slavery (albeit gradual) carried.
1795–7	Bill for abolition defeated.
1797	Published *Religious System of Professed Christians contrasted with Real Christianity*.
1798	Helped found the Church Missionary Society.
1803	Helped found the Bible Society.
1804	The Abolition Bill, which was carried through the House of Commons, was initially rejected by the Lords.
1807	Bill received Royal Assent.
	Founded the African Institution to put the Abolition Bill into practice.
1812–15	MP for Bramber.
1813	Involved in founding the Bishopric of Calcutta.

'They charge me with fanaticism. If to be feelingly alive to the sufferings of my fellow-creatures is to be a fanatic, I am one of the most incurable fanatics ever permitted to be at large.'

Speech, House of Commons, 19 June 1816

1823	Published *Appeal on Behalf of the Negro Slaves of the West Indies*.
DEATH	1833, aged 73, in London. Buried in Westminster Abbey.
HOBBIES & INTERESTS	The Church.

Duke of Wellington

Arthur Wellesley, British soldier popularly known as the Iron Duke, who proved to Europe that Napoleon could be beaten. He honed his skills in India, pushed the French out of Spain and won the Battle of Waterloo. He later became a Tory Prime Minister.

BIRTH 1769, Dublin, Ireland.

MARITAL STATUS Married, 1806, Hon. Katherine (Kitty) Sarah Dorothea Pakenham. Three sons and three daughters.

A Little Bit of Background

Napoleon was finally defeated by Wellington at the Battle of Waterloo in 1815. The Great Reform Bill was passed without Wellington in 1832. The Great Exhibition was staged in 1851.

EDUCATION Eton, Brussels, Angers Military Academy.

CAREER

1787	Lieutenant of Foot.
1787–93	Aide-de-camp in Ireland to Lord Lieutenant.
1790–5	MP for Trim in the Irish Parliament.
1792	Captain of Dragoons.
1793–1806	Lieutenant Colonel, 33rd Foot.
1794–5	Commanded 33rd Foot in Netherlands Campaign.
1797–1804	Commanded 33rd Foot in India.
1798	Changed the spelling of his name from Wesley to Wellesley.
1798–9	Command of troops at Vellore in India (the command obtained for him by his brother, the Viceroy).
1799	Command of a division in invasion of Mysore (the command again obtained for him by his brother).
1799–1802	Governor of Seringapatam and in charge of administration in Mysore.

1799–1800	Destroyed Dhoandiah Waugh.
1802	Major General.
1803	Commanded a division to restore the Peshwah.
1803–5	In charge of Deccan.
1803	Defeated the Mahrattas at the battles of Assaye and Argaum and Gawilghur.
	Made peace with Bevar and Scindiah.
1804	Destroyed the 'Pillagers of Perinda'.
	KB.
1806	Commanded a Brigade at Hastings.
1806–13	Colonel, 33rd Foot.
1806	MP for Rye, Sussex.
1807	MP for Mitchell.
1807	Defeated the Danes at Kioge.
1807–9	MP for Newport.
1807–9	Chief Secretary of Ireland.
1808	Lieutenant General.
	Command of a force sent to the Portuguese/Spanish Peninsula.
	Defeated Marshal Delaborde at Rolica.
	Defeated Marshal Junot at Vimeiro.
1809	Returned to England to face a Court Martial, but was acquitted and resumed his command.
1809	Chased Marshal Soult out of Oporto.
	Defeated Marshal Victor at Talavera.
	Devised lines of Torres Vedras, Portugal.
	Created Viscount Wellington.
1810	Defeated Marshal Massena at Busaco, Portugal.
1811	Chased Massena out of Portugal.
	Besieged Badajoz and Ciudad Rodrigo.
1812	Took Ciudad Rodrigo.
	Created Earl of Wellington.
1812	Took Badajoz.
	Defeated Marshal Marmont at the Arapiles Hills near Salamanca.
	Entered Madrid.
	Failed to take Burgos and retreated.
	Created Marquis of Wellington.

1813	Destroyed King Joseph's forces at Vitoria.
1813	Chased the French across the Pyrenees.
	Made Field Marshal.
	Knight of the Order of the Garter.
	Won the Battles of the Pyrenees. Took St Sebastian.
1814	Besieged Bayonne.
	Defeated Marshal Soult at Orthes and Toulouse.
	Created Duke of Wellington.
	Ambassador to Paris.
1815	Ambassador to Congress in Vienna.
	Assumed command of forces in Brussels.
	Defeated Napoleon at Waterloo.
	Advanced on Paris.
	GCB.

'Up Guards and at them!'

Quoted in a letter from an officer in the Guards, 22 June 1815, *The Battle of Waterloo* by a Near Observer (J. Booth), 1815, later denied by Wellington

'Hard pounding this, gentlemen; let's see who will pound longest.'

At the Battle of Waterloo, 1815, *Letters*, Sir Walter Scott Paul, letter 8, 1816,

'Ours is composed of the scum of the earth – the mere scum of the earth.'

Of the British Army, 4th November 1831, *Notes of Conversations with the Duke of Wellington*, Philip Henry Stanhope, 1888

All the business of war, and indeed all the business of life, is to endeavour to find out what you don't know by what you do; that's what I called 'guessing what was at the other side of the hill'.

The Croker Papers, vol. 3, ch. 28, 1885

1816	Headquartered at Cambray.
1817	Given Apsley House, London, and Strathfieldsaye by a grateful nation.

'Next to a battle lost, the greatest misery is a battle gained.'

Quoted in Diary of Frances, Lady Shelley, 1787–1817, vol. I, ch.9, ed. R. Edgcumbe, 1912;
Wellington made a similar remark many times

1818	Conference of Aix-la-Chapelle.
1818–27	Master-General of Ordnance.
1819–26	Governor of Plymouth.
1820–52	Lord Lieutenant of Hampshire.
1821/31/38	Lord High Constable at the Coronation of the monarch.
1824	Fought recognition of the Independence of Spain's American colonies.

'Publish and be damned.'

Attributed reply to a blackmail threat prior to the publication of Harriette Wilson's Memoirs,
1825, quoted in Wellington: The Years of the Sword, Elizabeth Longford, ch. 10, 1969

1826	Envoy to Tsar Nicholas of Russia over Greece.
1826–52	Constable of the Tower (of London).
1827–8	Commander-in-Chief.
1828–30	Prime Minister.

'An extraordinary affair. I gave them their orders and they wanted to stay and discuss them.'

Of his first Cabinet meeting as Prime Minister, attributed, Whitehall, Peter Hennessy, 1990

1829	Pushed Catholic Emancipation through Parliament (though he personally did not support it).
1830	Resigned as Prime Minister over Parliamentary reform.
1829–52	Lord Warden of the Cinque Ports.

'I used to say of him that his presence on the field made the difference of forty thousand men.'

Of Napoleon, 2nd November 1831, Notes of Conversations with the Duke of Wellington,
Philip Henry Stanhope, 1888

1834–52	Chancellor of Oxford University.

In my situation as Chancellor of the University of Oxford, I have been exposed to authors.

Collections and Recollections, G.W.E. Russell

1834	Prime Minister and Home Secretary.
1834	Foreign Secretary.
1835–41	Leader of the Conservative Opposition.
1840	Capital of New Zealand named after him.
1841–6	Cabinet Minister without Office.
1842–52	Commander-in-Chief.
1848	Advised Government on Chartist agitation for political reform.

'If you believe that, you'll believe anything.'

To a man who had accosted him in the street saying, 'Mr Jones, I believe?', *Pillar of State*, Elizabeth Longford, ch. 10, 1972

'You must build your House of Parliament upon the river . . . the populace cannot exact their demands by sitting down round you.'

Words on Wellington, William Fraser, 1889

DEATH	1852, aged 83, in Walmer, Kent. Buried in St Paul's Cathedral. Wellington College opened as his memorial in 1859.
HOBBIES & INTERESTS	Horses, the violin and boots. He received the first two pairs of his protoype 'riding half-boot' from his London cobbler in time for Waterloo – the Wellington boot.

William Wordsworth

Poet Laureate, inspired by his love of nature, whose attempts to create a less artificial and mannered poetry launched the Romantic movement.

BIRTH	1770, Cockermouth, Cumberland, son of an attorney.
MARITAL STATUS	Married, 1802, Mary Hutchinson, whom he'd known since childhood. Two sons, John and Thomas, who died young, and two daughters, Dora and Catherine, who also died young. One illegitimate daughter, Annette, the result of a youthful liaison with Annette Vallon, the daughter of a French surgeon.
EDUCATION	Hawkshead Grammar School and St John's College, Cambridge.

A Little Bit of Background

The French Revolution occurred in 1789, the same year in which Blake's *Songs of Innocence* were published. Coleridge published *The Ancient Mariner* in 1798. Jane Austen published *Pride and Prejudice* in 1813. The Penny Post was introduced in 1840.

CAREER

1790	Walking in Europe.
1792	Travelling in France 'imbibing Liberty'.
	Fell in love with Annette Vallon, the daughter of a surgeon at Blois, and had an illegitimate daughter.
1793	Published *An Evening Walk* and *Descriptive Sketches*.
1795	Received a legacy of £900 from his friend, Raisley Calvert.
1798	Published *Lyrical Ballads* with fellow poet Coleridge.
1798–9	Lived in Germany. Began his magnum opus, *The Prelude*.
1799–1850	Settled at Grasmere in the Lake District with his sister, Dorothy.

1801/3	Visited Scotland.
1802	Married.

> Poetry is the spontaneous overflow of powerful
> feelings: it takes its origin from emotion recollected
> in tranquillity.
>
> Preface, *Lyrical Ballads*, 2nd ed., 1802

1807	Published odes to *Duty* and *Liberty*.
	Intimations of Immortality.
	Miscellaneous Sonnets.

> Earth has not anything to show more fair:
> Dull would he be of soul who could pass by
> A sight so touching in its majesty:
> This City now doth like a garment wear
> The beauty of the morning; silent, bare,
> Ships, towers, domes, theatres, and temples lie
> Open unto the fields, and to the sky;
> All bright and glittering in the smokeless air.
>
> Dear God! The very houses seem asleep;
> And all that mighty heart is lying still!
>
> Composed upon Westminster Bridge, 1807
>
> Bliss was it in that dawn to be alive,
> But to be young was very heaven!
>
> The French Revolution, as it Appeared to Enthusiasts, 1809;
> also The Prelude, bk 9, l. 108, 1850

1813–42	Stamp Distributor for the County of Westmorland, a post which earned him £400 a year.
1814	Visited Scotland.
	Published *The Excursion*.

> I wandered lonely as a cloud
> That floats on high o'er vales and hills,
> When all at once I saw a crowd,
> A host, of golden daffodils;
> Beside the lake, beneath the trees,
> Fluttering and dancing in the breeze.
>
> *I wandered lonely as a cloud*, 1815 ed.

1819	Published *Peter Bell* and *The Waggoner*.
1820/3/8	Visited Europe.
1827	Left a legacy by Sir George Beaumont.
1829	Visited Ireland.
1831	Visited Scotland and the Isle of Man.
1833	Visited Scotland.
1837	Visited Europe.
1838	Hon. DCL Durham.
1839	Hon. DCL Oxford.
1842	Resigned from the Stamp Office and took a civil list pension of £300 per annum.
1843	Poet Laureate.
1850	*The Prelude* published posthumously.
DEATH	1850, aged 80, in Rydal Mount. Buried in St Oswald's Churchyard, Grasmere.
HOBBIES & INTERESTS	Nature.

Jane Austen

*Influential English novelist who exploited her quiet
middle-class life to produce gentle yet moving and
perceptive novels about relationships within a small society.*

BIRTH	1775, at Steventon Rectory, Hampshire, sixth youngest of seven. Her father was a clergyman.
MARITAL STATUS	Single.
EDUCATION	At home.

 ## A Little Bit of Background

Richardson's *Pamela* was published in 1741. Dr Johnson's
Dictionary came out in 1755. The Royal Crescent, Bath, was completed in
1775. Nelson was victorious at Trafalgar over the combined French and
Spanish fleets in 1805. Wellington won at Waterloo in 1815. Mary Shelley
wrote *Frankenstein* in 1818.

CAREER

1801	Moved from the family home to Bath after her father's retirement.
1806	Moved to Southampton following her father's death.
1809	Moved to Chawton, Hampshire, to live with her brother's family.
1811	Published *Sense and Sensibility*, at her own financial risk (she made a profit).

A man who has nothing to do with his own time has no
conscience in his intrusion on that of others.

Sense and Sensibility, vol. 2, ch. 9

1813	Published *Pride and Prejudice*.

Without thinking highly either of men or matrimony, marriage had always been her object; it was the only honourable provision for well-educated young women of small fortune, and however uncertain of giving happiness, must be their pleasantest preservative from want.

Pride and Prejudice, ch. 22

Loss of virtue in a female is irretrievable . . . one false step involves her in endless ruin.

Ibid., ch. 47

For what do we live, but to make sport for our neighbours, and laugh at them in our turn?

Ibid., ch. 57

1814	Published *Mansfield Park*.

Let other pens dwell on guilt and misery. I quit such odious subjects as soon as I can.

Mansfield Park, ch. 48

I think I may boast myself to be, with all possible vanity, the most unlearned and uninformed female who ever dared to be an authoress.

Letter, 11 December 1815, *Jane Austen's Letters*, ed. R.W. Chapman, 1952

1816	Published *Emma*.

I am going to make a heroine whom no-one but myself will much like.

On starting Emma, *A Memoir of Jane Austen*,
ed. J.E. Austen-Leigh, 1926 Emma, 1816, ch. 3

One half of the world cannot understand the pleasures of the other.

Emma, ch. 9

Surprises are foolish things. The pleasure is not enhanced, and the inconvenience is often considerable.

Ibid., ch. 26

1817 Moved to Winchester.

Single women have a dreadful propensity for being poor – which is one very strong argument in favour of matrimony.

Letter to Fanny Knight, 13 March 1817, *Jane Austen's Letters*, ed, R.W. Chapman, 1952

1818 *Northanger Abbey* and *Persuasion* published posthumously.

Oh! Who can ever be tired of Bath?

Northanger Abbey, ch. 10

'My idea of good company, Mr Elliot, is the company of clever, well-informed people, who have a great deal of conversation; that is what I call good company.' 'You are mistaken,' said he gently, 'that is not good company, that is the best.'

Persuasion, ch. 16

All the privilege I claim for my own sex . . . is that of loving longest, when existence or when hope is gone.

Ibid., ch. 23

DEATH 1817, aged 41, at Winchester, of Addison's disease. Buried in Winchester Cathedral.

HOBBIES & INTERESTS Her family, friends and neighbours.

J.M.W. Turner

Joseph Mallord William Turner, English landscape painter of great originality, whose use of light and colour anticipated the Impressionists.

BIRTH	1775, Covent Garden, London, the son of a barber.
MARITAL STATUS	Single. Two daughters by a mistress, Sarah Danby.
EDUCATION	1789, Royal Academy School. Studied under Sir Joshua Reynolds.

 ## A Little Bit of Background

The Royal Academy was founded in 1769 and Sir Joshua Reynolds was its first President. Gainsborough painted *The Blue Boy* in 1770 and Constable his *Haywain* in 1821. Robert Stephenson built his steam engine, *The Rocket*, in 1829.

CAREER	
1790	Exhibited at the Royal Academy for first time, *A view of Lambeth Palace.*
	Visited the North of England.
1800–20	Painted in the style of the old masters.
1807	Painted *Sun rising through vapour.*
1808	Royal Academy Professor of Perspective.
	Travelled in the North of England, Scotland and Europe.
1820–35	Abandoned his attempts to imitate the old masters and aimed instead at 'ideal compositions'.
1828	Visited France and Italy.
1829	Painted *Ulysses deriding Polyphemus.*
1832	Visited Venice.
1835	Adopted his own style, trying to 'speak' in a 'colour language'.

J.M. W. Turner

1839	Painted *The Fighting Téméraire*.
1844	Painted *Rain, Steam and Speed*.

'He sees more in my pictures than I ever painted!'

On the art critic John Ruskin, *Sunny Memories*, Mary Lloyd, vol. 1, 1879

'If I could find anything blacker than black, I'd use it.'

When a friend complained of the blackness of the sails in *Peace – Burial at Sea*, 1844, quoted in *Dictionary of National Biography*, 1917

'I did not expect to escape, but I felt bound to record it if I did.'

Of watching a storm at sea, while on board a Margate steamer, ibid.

'I've lost one of my children this week.'

Having just sold a painting, ibid.

'My business is to paint not what I know but what I see.'

In answer to a complaint that the ships in one of his pictures had no portholes, ibid.

DEATH	1851, aged 75, in Cheyne Walk, Chelsea, London. Buried in St Paul's Cathedral.
HOBBIES & INTERESTS	The weather.

 # John Constable

English landscape painter with a particular love of the Essex and Suffolk countryside.

BIRTH	1776, East Bergholt, Suffolk, the son of a miller.
MARITAL STATUS	Married, 1816, Maria Bicknell, d. 1829, of tuberculosis. Seven children.
EDUCATION	Dedham School, Essex. 1795–7 art student in London.

 ## A Little Bit of Background

The Royal Academy was founded in 1769. Turner's *Sun rising through vapour* was painted in 1807. War with France ended in 1815.

CAREER	
1799	Lived in London.
1802	Exhibited a landscape at the Royal Academy.
1804/9	Painted two altarpieces.
1803–37	Painted English landscapes, including *The Haywain*.
1824	Fêted by the French Salon of painters.
1828	Came into an inheritance, which enabled him to devote himself to his unremunerative landscape painting.
1829	Royal Academy.
1833	Many of his landscapes engraved.
1833–6	Lectured on 'Landscape Art'.

The sound of water escaping from mill-dams, etc., willows, old rotten planks, slimy posts and brickwork . . . those scenes made me a painter and I am grateful.

Letter to John Fisher, 23 October 1821, *Memoirs of the Life of John Constable*, C.R. Leslie ch. 5, 1843

A gentleman's park – is my aversion. It is not beauty because it
is not nature.

Of Fonthill; letter to John Fisher, 7 October 1822, *Correspondence*, vol. 6, 1968

There is nothing ugly; I never saw an ugly thing in my life;
for let the form of an object be what it may, – light, shade, and
perspective will always make it beautiful.

Memoirs of the Life of John Constable, C.R. Leslie, ch. 17, 1843

DEATH | 1837, aged 60, in London. Buried beside his wife in St John's, Church Row, Hampstead.

HOBBIES & INTERESTS | Fishing.

Elizabeth Fry

English Quaker and prison reformer whose religious beliefs compelled her to improve the lot of prisoners throughout Britain and also in Europe.

BIRTH   1780, as Elizabeth Gurney, Earlham, Norfolk.

MARITAL STATUS   Married, 1800, Joseph Fry. Twelve children.

EDUCATION   At home.

A Little Bit of Background

George Fox founded the Society of Friends, known as the Quakers, in 1648. Convicts were transported to Australia from 1788. Florence Nightingale revolutionised nursing during the Crimean War, 1854–6. Thomas Barnardo established his first home for destitute children in 1870, and by the time of his death in 1905 his foundation had helped over 60,000.

CAREER

1800	Married Joseph Fry.
1809	Became a Quaker minister.
1817	The plight of women prisoners at Newgate led her to form a prison improvement association.
1818	Persuaded the Government to improve conditions for convicts being transported to the colonies.
1832	Received by King of Prussia.
1833	Founded an Order of Nurses.
1834	Helped homeless in London and Brighton.

Does capital punishment tend to the security of the people?
By no means. It hardens the hearts of men, and makes the loss of
life appear light to them; and it renders life insecure, inasmuch as
the law holds out that property is of greater value than life.

Note found among her papers, *Memoir of the Life of Elizabeth Fry*,
Rachel E. Cresswell and Katharine Fry, 1848

Punishment is not for revenge, but to lessen crime and reform
the criminal.

Ibid.

DEATH	1845, aged 65, in Ramsgate. Buried in the Friends Burial Ground, Barking.
HOBBIES & INTERESTS	The poor.

George Stephenson

Inventor and railway pioneer who designed the world's first practical railway locomotive, Locomotion.

BIRTH	1781, Wylam, Newcastle, son of a colliery fireman.
MARITAL STATUS	Married first, 1802, Frances 'Fanny' Henderson, d. 1806. Their son, Robert, was also a railway engineer. Secondly, Elizabeth Hindley, d. 1845.
EDUCATION	Self-educated: could barely read.

 ## A Little Bit of Background

The Cornishman Thomas Savory built the first steam pump in 1698. The design was improved by James Watt in 1769, who added a separate condenser. In 1814, William Hedley built *Puffing Billy* for pulling coal.

CAREER	Worked at the same colliery as his father.
1802	Engine man at Willington Ballast Hill.
1804	Worked at Killingworth Colliery.
1807	Worked at Montrose Colliery
1808	Went back to Killingworth.
1812	Promoted to Enginewright at Killingworth Colliery.
1814	First successful locomotive trials.
1815	Patented his steam blast engine.
	Designed a safety lamp, similar to that designed by Humphry Davy at the same time.
1818	Received a testimonial and £1,000.
1819–23	Laid railway for Hetton Colliery.
1824	Engineer for Stockton and Darlington Railway, which opened in 1825, where his engine, *Locomotion*, achieved a speed of 15 mph.
	Surveyed Manchester and Liverpool rail route.

1826	Appointed Engineer for the Liverpool and Manchester Railway, which opened in 1830.
1829	*Rocket*, designed and built for him by his son Robert, won the Rainhill trials and a prize of £500.

> I see no reason to suppose that these machines will ever force themselves into general use.
>
> Duke of Wellington

1833	Chief Engineer to Birmingham, Manchester, Liverpool line.
1835	Knighted by Leopold I of Belgium, but refused any British honours because he felt unworthy of them.
1836	Chief Engineer to Northern Lines.
1837	Chief Engineer Derby–Leeds Railway. Achieved 29 mph by application of the Gurney steam jet.
1838	Vice President British Association (Mechanical Science Section).
1844	Attempted to calm 'railway mania', the frenzied investment in railway shares and land on which railways might be built, through a series of talks, lectures and private meetings.
1847	First President of the Institution of Mechanical Engineers.
DEATH	1848, aged 67, at Tapton House Chesterfield.
HOBBIES & INTERESTS	Maps.

Lord Palmerston

Henry John Temple, British statesman and Prime Minister,
1855–8 and 1859–65, a Member of Parliament for almost
50 years and an advocate of 'gunboat diplomacy'.

BIRTH   1784, No. 4 Park Street, Westminster (now No. 20, Queen Anne's Gate) .

MARITAL STATUS   Married, 1839, Lady Cowper.

EDUCATION   Harrow, Edinburgh and St John's College, Cambridge.

 ## A Little Bit of Background

There was a revolution in Paris in 1830. The Reform Act, the beginning of modern democracy as we know it, was passed in 1832, the same year that Greece gained Independence from the Turks. Britain gained Hong Kong in the first Opium War with China in 1842. 1848 was the year of revolutions in Europe. The Crimean War began in 1854 and ended in 1856. The Indian Mutiny erupted in 1857. America descended into a four-year civil war in 1861.

CAREER

1802	Became Third Viscount Palmerston.
1807	Tory MP for Newport, Isle of Wight.
1808	Lord of the Admiralty.
1809–28	Secretary at War.
1811–31	MP for Cambridge University.
1818	Wounded in assassination attempt.
1829	First great speech on foreign affairs.
1830	'Crossed the floor' to become a Whig.
1830–41	Foreign Secretary.
1839	Sent gunboats to Canton to defend the Opium trade.

. . . created Belgium, saved Portugal and Spain from absolutism, rescued Turkey from Russia, and the highway to India from France

1841–6	In Opposition.
1846–51	Foreign Secretary, saved Switzerland from France and Austria.

'We have no eternal allies and we have no perpetual enemies. Our interests are eternal and perpetual, and those interests it is our duty to follow.' Speech, House of Commons, 1 March 1848

1850	Compelled Greece to accept his terms in the Pacifico affair, an event that polarised attitudes to British foreign policy.

'I therefore fearlessly challenge the verdict which this House . . . is to give . . . whether, as the Roman, in days of old, held himself free from indignity, when he could say Civis Romanus sum; so also a British subject, in whatever land he may be, shall feel confident that the watchful eye and the strong arm of England will protect him against injustice and wrong.'

Speech, House of Commons, 25 June 1850, during the debate on the protection afforded to the Athens trader Don Pacifico, a Portuguese Jew who had been born a British subject in Gilbraltar, after an anti-Semitic crowd had burnt his house in 1847

1852	Home Secretary.
1855–65	Prime Minister.
1856	Knight of the Order of the Garter.

We do not want Egypt any more than any rational man with an estate in the north of England and a residence in the south, would have wished to possess the inns on the north road. All he could want would have been that the inns should be well kept, always accessible, and furnishing him, when he came, with mutton chops and post horses.

Letter to Earl Cowley, 25 November 1859, *Life of . . . Viscount Palmerston*, 1846–65, Hon. Evelyn Ashley, vol. 2, ch. 4, 1876

1861	Warden of Cinque Ports.
	Maintained British neutrality during the American Civil War.
1863	Lord Rector of Glasgow University.
	Cited in a divorce case.

The function of a government is to calm, rather than to excite agitation.

Gladstone and Palmerston, P. Guedalla, 1928

'How d'ye do, and how is the old complaint?'

Reputed greeting to all those he did not know, *Recollections*, A. West, vol. 1, ch. 2, 1899

Lord Palmerston . . . said that only three men in Europe had ever understood [the Schleswig-Holstein question], and of these the Prince Consort was dead, a Danish statesman (unnamed) was in an asylum, and he himself had forgotten it.

Britain in Europe 1789–1914, R.W. Seton-Watson, 1937, ch. 11, 1937

DEATH	1865, aged 81, at Brocket Hall, Hertfordshire. Buried in Westminster Abbey.

'Die, my dear Doctor, that's the last thing I shall do.'

Last words

HOBBIES & INTERESTS	Dancing, hunting, trying new false teeth.

Lord Byron

*George Gordon Byron, handsome English Romantic poet
and rake, author of* Childe Harold *and* Don Juan, *whose
relations with women, including his half-sister Augusta,
scandalised London society, causing him to spend the latter
part of his life abroad.*

BIRTH	1788, London, with what is thought to have been a club foot.
MARITAL STATUS	Married, 1815, Anne Isabella Milbanke, separated 1816. One daughter Ada. One illegitimate daughter, Allegra, b. 1817, by his mistress Claire Clairmont. Also possibly another illegitimate daughter by his half-sister, Augusta.
EDUCATION	Aberdeen Grammar School, Harrow and Trinity College, Cambridge, where he kept a bear in his room.

 A Little Bit of Background

Wellington won the Battle of Waterloo in 1815. Keats
published *Ode to a Nightingale* in 1820. Greece finally gained
Independence from the Turks in 1832.

CAREER

1798	Inherited the family title and bankrupt estate, Newstead Abbey, near Nottingham.
1806	*Fugitive Pieces* was privately printed, republished as *Hours of Idleness*, 1807.

> Friendship is Love without his wings!
>
> *L'Amitié est l'amour sans ailes,* written 1806, published 1831

1809	Took seat in House of Lords. Issued *English Bards and Scotch Reviewers*.

1809 Rode from Lisbon to Cadiz. Visited Gibraltar, Malta, Greece and Turkey.

1810 Swam the Hellespont, a narrow strait in north-west Turkey connecting the Aegean Sea and the Sea of Marmara.

1812 Spoke twice in the House of Lords.

A land of meanness, sophistry, and mist.

Of Scotland, *The Curse of Minerva*, 138, 1812

1812 Published cantos I and II of *Childe Harold's Pilgrimage*.

'I awoke one morning and found myself famous.'

On the instantaneous success of *Childe Harold*,
Letters and Journals of Lord Byron,
Thomas Moore, vol. 1, 1830

Cold is the heart, fair Greece! That looks on thee,
Nor feels as lovers o'er the dust they loved;
Dull is the eye that will not weep to see
Thy walls defaced, thy mouldering shrines removed
By British hands.

Childe Harold's Pilgrimage, canto II, st. 15

1812 Wrecked his health on quack diets trying to lose weight.

1815 Married Miss Milbanke.

'You should have a softer pillow than my heart.'

To his wife, who had rested her head on his breast,
The Life and Letters of Anne Isabella, Lady Noel Byron,
ed. E.C. Mayne, ch. 11, 1929

1816 Accused of insanity by his wife, who left him.
Travelled in Europe, Belgium, the Rhine, Geneva. Wrote *Childe Harold*, canto III.

The wondering outlaw of his own dark mind.

Childe Harold's Pilgrimage, canto III, st. 3

> On with the dance! Let joy be unconfined;
> No sleep till morn, when Youth and Pleasure meet
> To chase the glowing Hours with flying feet.
>
> *Ibid., canto III, st. 22*

1816   Wintered in Venice.
1817   Fathered a daughter, Augusta.
Visited Rome, stayed in Venice.
Wrote *Childe Harold*, canto IV.
1819–21 Wrote *Don Juan*, cantos I–V.

> What men call gallantry, and gods adultery,
> Is much more common where the climate's sultry.
>
> *Don Juan, canto I, st. 63*
>
> Pleasure's a sin, and sometimes sin's a pleasure.
>
> *Ibid., canto I, st. 133*
>
> In her first passion woman loves her lover,
> In all the others all she loves is love.
>
> *Ibid., canto III, st. 3*

1819   Stayed in Ravenna, Italy, and wrote dramas.
1821–4 Wrote the concluding cantos of *Don Juan*.

> And, after all, what is a lie? 'Tis but
> The truth in masquerade.
>
> *Ibid., canto XI, st. 37*
>
> Now hatred is by far the longest pleasure;
> Men love in haste, but they detest at leisure.
>
> *Ibid., canto XIII, st. 4*
>
> 'Tis strange – but true; for truth is always strange;
> Stranger than fiction.
>
> *Ibid., canto XIV, st. 101*

1822–3	Founded *The Liberal* newspaper.
	Moved to Genoa.
1823	Sailed from Genoa to join Greek insurgents.
1824	Enlisted a Greek regiment, which he disbanded on the grounds of their 'lethargy and impudence'.
DEATH	1824, aged 36, from marsh fever at Ayios Georgios, Greece. Buried in the Byron Vault at Hucknall Torkard, Nottingham. Memorial in Westminster Abbey.
HOBBIES & INTERESTS	Dieting, cricket and swimming.

Sir Robert Peel

*British Prime Minister, founder of the Conservative Party
and of the first civilian police force, who repealed the Corn
Laws, but was broken by his failure to alleviate the Irish
Potato Famine.*

BIRTH	1788, Bury, Lancashire, son of a cotton manufacturer.
MARITAL STATUS	Married, 1820, Julia Floyd. Five sons and two daughters.
EDUCATION	Harrow and Christ Church, Oxford.

A Little Bit of Background

The Peterloo Massacre, when Manchester magistrates ordered troops to clear a peaceful crowd of 60,000 demanding the reform of Parliament, resulting in some 500 being injured and 11 killed, occurred in 1819. The Reform Act of 1832, the beginning of democracy as we know it, extended the electorate and reformed Parliament. The Irish Potato Famine was at its height in 1845–6.

CAREER

1809	Tory MP for Cashel (the seat having been bought for him by his father).
1810–12	Under Secretary for War and the Colonies.
1812–18	Chief Secretary for Ireland.
1815	Established the Peace Preservation Police – the 'Peelers' or 'Bobbies', unarmed and dressed in blue to distinguish them from the army.
1815	Branded a 'coward and cad' for refusing to give Irish politician Daniel O'Connell 'satisfaction' in a duel over Catholic emancipation, which he opposed.
1817	MP for Oxford University.

| 1822 | Home Secretary. |
| 1827 | Resigned as Home Secretary. |

'There is not a single law connected with my name which has not had as its object some mitigation of the severity of the criminal law; some prevention of abuse in the exercise of it; or some security for its impartial administration.'

Speech, House of Commons, 1 May 1827

| 1828 | Home Secretary and Leader of the House of Commons. |
| 1829 | MP for Westbury. |

'As minister of the Crown . . . I reserve to myself, distinctly and unequivocally, the right of adapting my conduct to the exigency of the moment, and to the wants of the country.'   Ibid., 30 March 1829

All my experience in public life is in favour of the employment of what the world would call young men instead of old ones.

To the Duke of Wellington, 1829, *Sir Robert Peel*, Norman Gash, 2nd ed., 1986

| 1830 | MP for Tamworth, Staffordshire. |

'The hasty inordinate demand for peace might be just as dangerous as the clamour of war.'

Speech, House of Commons, 1832

'I see no dignity in persevering in error.'

Ibid., 1833

| 1834 | Transformed the Tory Party into the modern Conservative Party and was subsequently elected Prime Minister, First Lord of the Treasury and Chancellor of the Exchequer. |

'Of all vulgar arts of government, that of solving every difficulty which might arise by thrusting the hand into the public purse is the most delusory and contemptible.'

Ibid., 1834

1835	Resigned after being defeated by a coalition of Whigs, radicals and Irish nationalists.
1841–6	Re-elected Prime Minister.
1846	Repealed the Corn Laws, partly in response to the famine in Ireland, but in doing so disaffected Conservative landowners and as a result was deserted by his party.
DEATH	1850, aged 62, from injuries sustained following a fall from his horse on Constitution Hill, London.
HOBBIES & INTERESTS	The Law.

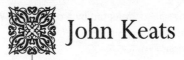

John Keats

Author of Ode to a Nightingale, *who trained as a doctor but devoted his short adult life to poetry.*

BIRTH	1795, son of a livery stable keeper from Moorfields, London.
MARITAL STATUS	Single. Exchanged love letters with Fanny Brawne, his next-door neighbour.
EDUCATION	Taught by John Clarke at Enfield.
CAREER	
1816	Dresser at Guy's Hospital, having been apprenticed to a surgeon.
	Published the sonnet *On first looking into Chapman's Homer.*

> Then felt I like some watcher of the skies
> When a new planet swims into his ken;
> Or like stout Cortez when with eagle eyes
> He stared at the Pacific — and all his men
> Looked at each other with a wild surmise —
> Silent, upon a peak in Darien.
>
> *On first looking into Chapman's Homer*

1817	Published *Sonnets.*
	Published *Poems by John Keats*, with the help of Shelley.
	Lived with his brothers in Hampstead.

> I am certain of nothing but the holiness of the heart's affections and the truth of imagination — what the imagination seizes as beauty must be truth — whether it existed before or not.
>
> Letter to Benjamin Bailey, 8 October 1817, *Letters of John Keats*, ed. H.E. Rollins, vol. 1, 1958

1818	Published *Endymion*, having earlier recited part of it to Wordsworth.
	Started *Hyperion*.
	Nursed his brother, Tom, who was dying of tuberculosis.

If poetry comes not as naturally as the leaves to a tree it had better not come at all.

Letter to John Taylor, 27 February 1818, *Letters of John Keats*, ed. H.E. Rollins, vol. 1, 1958

Scenery is fine — but human nature is finer.   Ibid.

1820	*Ode to a Nightingale*, *Ode to a Grecian Urn*, *To Autumn*, *The Eve of St Agnes* and *La Belle Dame sans Merci* all published, only seven months before his death.

'Beauty is truth, truth beauty,' — that is all
Ye know on earth, and all ye need to know.

Ode to a Grecian Urn, st. 5

My heart aches, and a drowsy numbness pains
My sense, as though of hemlock I had drunk,
Or emptied some dull opiate to the drains . . .

Ode to a Nightingale, st. 1

Season of mists and mellow fruitfulness,
Close bosom-friend of the maturing sun;
Conspiring with him how to load and bless
With fruit the vines that round the thatch-eaves run.

To Autumn, st. 1

1820	Sailed for Italy for his health.
DEATH	1821, aged 25, of consumption (tuberculosis), in Rome. Buried in the Protestant Cemetery, Rome.
HOBBIES & INTERESTS	Medicine.

Benjamin Disraeli

First Earl of Beaconsfield, novelist and Conservative Prime Minister of Italian-Jewish descent who made Queen Victoria Empress of India.

BIRTH

1804, in Bedford Row, Camden, London, eldest son of Isaac D'Israeli who, although a Jew, had his children baptised as Christians, thus enabling his son to have a political career (Jews were unable to sit in the House of Commons until legislation introduced in 1858 by Disraeli himself).

MARITAL STATUS

Married, 1839, Mary Anne Lewis (née Evans), a widow 12 years his senior.

EDUCATION

Higham Hall School, Walthamstow, a private Unitarian school, and in his father's library.

 A Little Bit of Background

Queen Victoria came to the throne in 1837. The Crimean War lasted from 1854 to 1856, and the Indian Mutiny from 1857 to 1858. Architect Charles Barry's Houses of Parliament opened in 1860. The first Gilbert & Sullivan operetta, *Trial by Jury*, was performed in 1875. W.G. Grace scored the first ever test century against Australia in 1880.

CAREER

1824 Entered Lincoln's Inn.

1826 Published *Vivian Grey*, his first novel, anonymously, to pay off debts. It was received with huge acclaim.

> There is no act of treachery or meanness of which a political party is not capable; for in politics there is no honour.
>
> *Vivian Grey*, bk 4, ch. 1

1828 Travelled in Spain.

1831	Travelled in Italy.
	Published *The Young Duke*.
1832	Published *Contarini Fleming*.

> Read no history: nothing but biography, for that is life without theory.
>
> *Contarini Fleming*, pt. 1, ch . 23

1833	Published *Alroy*.
1834	Published *The Rise of Iskander*.
1835	Wrote *A Vindication of the British Constitution*.
1837	Published *Venetia*.
	Published *Henrietta Temple*.
	Elected MP for Maidstone (and as such could not be imprisoned for debt) and supported the political reformers the Chartists.

> 'Though I sit down now, the time will come when you will hear me.'
>
> Maiden speech, House of Commons,
> which was howled down, 7 December 1837

> 'The Continent will [not] suffer England to be the workshop of the world.'
>
> Speech, House of Commons, 15 March 1838

1839	Married a wealthy widow, thus securing himself a reliable income and a large house.
1841	Conservative MP for Shrewsbury. Supported the Corn Laws, an attempt to ensure a sufficient home-grown supply by regulating imports and exports.
1844	Published *Coningsby; or The New Generation*.

> 'Thus you have a starving population, an absentee aristocracy, and an alien Church, and in addition the weakest executive in the world. That is the Irish Question.'
>
> Ibid., 16 February 1844

Youth is a blunder; Manhood a struggle; Old Age a regret.

Coningsby, bk 3, ch. 1

1845   Published *Sybil; or The Two Nations*.

'Two nations; between whom there is no intercourse and no sympathy; who are as ignorant of each other's habits, thoughts, and feelings, as if they were dwellers in different zones, or inhabitants of different planets; who are formed by a different breeding, are fed by a different food, are ordered by different manners, and are not governed by the same laws.'
'You speak of – ' said Egremont, hesitatingly.
'THE RICH AND THE POOR.'

Sybil, bk 2, ch. 5

1847   Published *Tancred*.
1847–76   MP for Buckinghamshire.

'Justice is truth in action.'

Speech, House of Commons, 11 February 1851

1852   Chancellor of the Exchequer.
1858–9   Chancellor of the Exchequer and Leader of the House of Commons.

'Party is organised opinion.'

Speech, Oxford University, 25 November 1864,
quoted in *The Times*, 26 November 1864

'Is man an ape or an angel? Now I am on the side of the angels.'

Ibid.

1866   Chancellor of the Exchequer.
1867   Carried Bill giving all rate payers the vote.
1868   Prime Minister.
1870   Published *Lothair*.

> A Protestant, if he wants aid or advice on any matter, can only go to his solicitor.
>
> *Lothair*, ch. 27

1874–80 Prime Minister.
1876 Persuaded Queen Victoria to accept the title of Empress of India.
Created Earl of Beaconsfield.

> 'I am dead; dead, but in the Elysian fields.'
>
> *Life of Benjamin Disraeli,*
> W. Monypenny and G. Buckle, vol. 5, ch. 13, 1920

1878 Attended Congress of Berlin, where he achieved 'peace with honour'.
KG (Knight of the Order of the Garter).

> 'A sophistical rhetorician, inebriated with the exuberance of his own verbosity.'
>
> Of his Liberal rival Gladstone, quoted in *The Times*, 29 July 1878

1879 Occupied Cyprus.
1880 Published *Endymion* (for which he was paid £10,000, then an enormous amount of money).

> 'Sensible men are all of the same religion.' 'And pray what is that?'
> ' . . . Sensible men never tell.'
>
> *Endymion*, ch. 81

> 'Everyone likes flattery; and when you come to Royalty you should lay it on with a trowel.'
>
> To Matthew Arnold, *Collections and Recollections*, G.W.E. Russell, ch. 23, 1898

> 'Damn your principles! Stick to your party.'
>
> Attributed to Disraeli and believed to have been said to Edward Bulwer-Lytton,
> *Famous Sayings and their Authors*, E. Latham, 1904

'When I want to read a novel, I write one.'

> Comment made on the publication of *Daniel Deronda*,
> *Life of Benjamin Disraeli*, W. Monypenny and G. Buckle,
> vol. 6, ch. 17, 1920

'Never complain and never explain.'

> *Life of William Ewart Gladstone*, J. Morley, vol. 1, 1903

'There are three kinds of lies: lies, damned lies and statistics.'

> Attributed to Disraeli in *Autobiography*, Mark Twain, vol. 1, 1924

'No it is better not. She would only ask me to take a message to Albert.'

> On his deathbed, declining a proposed visit from Queen Victoria,
> *Disraeli*, Robert Blake, ch. 32, 1966

DEATH | 1881, aged 76, in London. Buried at Hughenden Manor, Buckinghamshire.

HOBBIES & INTERESTS | Luxury.

Isambard Kingdom Brunel

Innovator and engineer who built and designed every detail of the Great Western Railway.

BIRTH   1806, in Portsmouth, son of a French-born engineer. He was raised in Normandy, France.

MARITAL STATUS   Married, 1836, Mary Horsley. Two sons, Isambard and Henry Marc, and one daughter, Florence.

EDUCATION   At home and in Paris.

 ## A Little Bit of Background

The Bridgewater Canal, built to take coal from Worsley to Manchester, was opened in 1761. Richard Trevithick invented the self-propelled engine in 1804. The Stockton and Darlington Railway opened in 1825. The Great Exhibition was held in 1851.

CAREER

1825   His father's clerk.

1826   Resident Engineer of the Thames Tunnel, between Wapping and Rotherhithe, the world's first underwater tunnel.

1830   Designed the Clifton Suspension Bridge.

> 'Why is it beautiful? Because it works.'
> Reputedly said to a mill owner, about the Clifton Suspension Bridge

1833   Chief Engineer to the Great Western Railway.

1836   Married.

1845–52   Fitted screw propellers to steamships. Designed and built the *Great Western*, the first steamship to make transatlantic crossings and the iron-hulled *Great Britain*.

1852–8   Designed the *Great Eastern* steamship, then the largest in the world.

1852–8	Improved artillery design.
DEATH	1859, aged 55, of a stroke on board the *Great Eastern*, just before her maiden voyage. Buried in Kensal Green Cemetery.
HOBBIES & INTERESTS	Cigars and magic tricks.

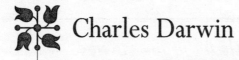 # Charles Darwin

Naturalist, author of The Origin of Species *and* The Descent of Man, *whose theory of evolution by natural selection stunned the scientific community and caused many to question the literal truth of the Bible.*

BIRTH   1809 in Shrewsbury. His mother was the daughter of Josiah Wedgwood.

MARITAL STATUS   Married, 1839, Emma Wedgwood, his cousin. Six sons and four daughters.

EDUCATION   Shrewsbury Grammar School, Edinburgh University, where he studied medicine, and Christ's College, Cambridge, with a view to entering the Church.

CAREER

1831   Travelled as the official 'naturalist' on board HMS *Beagle* on a scientific expedition to South America.

1836   Returned to England.

1840   Published *Journal of Researches into the Geology and Natural History of the various countries visited by HMS Beagle.*

1838–41   Secretary to the Geographical Society.

1844   Wrote *The Volcanic Islands.*

1859   Published *On the Origin of Species by means of Natural Selection, or the Preservation of favoured races in the struggle for life.* All 1,250 copies printed were sold on the first day.

> I have called this principle, by which each slight variation, if useful, is preserved, by the term of Natural Selection.
>
> *The Origin of Species*, ch. 3, 1859

> ### A Little Bit of Background
>
> The philosophers Karl Marx (1818–93) and Friedrich Nietzsche (1844–1900) were firmly anti-religious. The first whole Neanderthal skeleton was unearthed in France in 1908. The word 'agnostic' was coined by Thomas Huxley to describe Darwin.

The expression often used by Mr Herbert Spencer of the Survival of the Fittest is more accurate (than 'Struggle for Existence'), and is sometime equally convenient.

The Origin of Species, ch. 3, 1869 ed.

There is a grandeur in this view of life.

The Origin of Species, ch. 14, 1859

1868	Published *Variation of Animals* and *Plants under Domestication*.
1871	Published *The Descent of Man, and selection in relation to sex*.

Man with all his noble qualities . . . still bears in his bodily frame the indelible stamp of his lowly origin.

The Descent of Man, concluding words

1872–9	Published other material, mainly on the evolution of plants.
DEATH	1882, aged 73, in Downe, Kent, of a heart attack. Buried in Westminster Abbey.
HOBBIES & INTERESTS	Tortoises and finches.

William Gladstone

Devout Liberal statesman, Prime Minister 1868–74, 1880–4, 1886 and 1892–4, who was determined to bring peace to Ireland and education to all.

BIRTH	1809, in Liverpool, fourth son of a Liverpool merchant and MP.
MARITAL STATUS	Married, 1839, Catherine Glynne. Eight children.
EDUCATION	Eton and Christ Church, Oxford.

A Little Bit of Background

Queen Victoria was on the throne from 1837 to 1901. The Great Exhibition was held in 1851. The Crimean War lasted from 1854 to 1856, and the Indian Mutiny from 1857 to 1858. Irish Home Rule Bills were rejected in 1886 and 1893.

CAREER

1830	President of the Oxford Union.
1831	Double first in Classics and Mathematics.
1832	Conservative MP for Newark.
1833	Entered Lincoln's Inn.
1834	Junior Lord of the Treasury.
1835	Under-Secretary for War and the Colonies.
	Elected Conservative MP for Newark.
1837	Re-elected Conservative MP for Newark.
1838	Published *The State in its Relations with the Church*.
1840	Published *Church principles considered in their results*.
	Opposed the first Opium War with China, which was intended to protect the lucrative opium trade of the East India Company.
1841–5	Re-elected Conservative MP for Newark.

1841	Vice-President of Board of Trade. Master of the Mint. Privy Councillor.
1843	President of the Board of Trade.
1845	Resigned office and published *Remarks on Recent Commercial Legislation.*

> Ireland, Ireland! That cloud in the west, that coming storm.
>
> Letter to his wife, 12 October 1845

1845–6	Secretary of State for Colonies.
1847–65	'Peelite' MP for Oxford University.
1851	Chancellor of the Exchequer.
1853	First Budget.
1854	Second Budget.
1855	Resigned office when Palmerston became Prime Minister.
1858	Published *Studies on Homer and the Homeric Age.*

> Finance is, as it were, the stomach of the country, from which all the other organs take their tone.
>
> Article on finance, 1858, *Gladstone 1809–1874*, H.C.G. Matthew, ch. 5, 1986

1859–66	Chancellor of the Exchequer.
1860	Lord Rector of Edinburgh University.
1865–8	MP for South Lancashire.
1865	Leader of the House.

> 'You cannot fight against the future. Time is on our side.'
>
> Speech on the Reform Bill, House of Commons, 27 April 1866

1867	Leader of the Liberal Party.
1868–74	MP for Greenwich. Prime Minister.

> 'My mission is to pacify Ireland.'
>
> On receiving news that he was to form his first cabinet, 1 December 1868, *Gladstone 1809–1874*, H.C.G. Matthew, ch. 5, 1986

Swimming for his life, a man does not see much of the country through which the river winds.

31 December 1868, *The Gladstone Diaries*, ed. M.R.D. Foot and H.C.G. Matthew, vol. 6, 1978

1869	Published *Juventus Mundi*.
1873	Prime Minister and Chancellor of the Exchequer.
1875	Resigned leadership of the Liberal Party.
1876	Published *Homeric Synchronism*.
1877	Lord Rector of Glasgow University.
1880	MP for Midlothian. Prime Minister.
1880–2	Chancellor of the Exchequer.

'Ideal perfection is not the true basis of English legislation. We look at the attainable; we look at the practical, and we have too much English sense to be drawn away by those sanguine delineations of what might possibly be attained in Utopia, from a path which promises to enable us to effect great good for the people of England.'

Speech on the Reform Bill, House of Commons, 28 February 1884

1885	Rejected an earldom.
1886	Prime Minister.
1892–4	Prime Minister and Lord Privy Seal.
1895	Resigned as MP.

What that Sicilian mule was to me, I have been to the Queen.

Of a mule on which Gladstone rode, which he 'could neither love nor like', although it had rendered him 'much valuable service', memorandum, 20 March 1894, *The Gladstone Diaries*, H.C.G. Matthew, vol. 8, 1994

Money should fructify in the pockets of the people.

Gladstone 1809–1874, H.C.G. Matthew, 1986

DEATH	19 May 1898, aged 89, at Hawarden Castle, Flint. Buried in Westminster Abbey.
HOBBIES & INTERESTS	Saving fallen women, chopping wood and Ancient Greek.

William Makepeace Thackeray

Journalist and novelist, author of Vanity Fair.

BIRTH

1811, in Calcutta. An only child, his father, a Collector for the East India Company, died when he was three.

MARITAL STATUS

Married, 1836, Isabella Shawe. Separated 1840, after she became insane. Three daughters, one of whom died shortly after birth.

EDUCATION

Charterhouse and Trinity College, Cambridge, where he ran up gambling debts and left without taking a degree. Also attended a London art school and a Paris atelier.

A Little Bit of Background

Wellington won at Waterloo in 1815. Charles Dickens published *Pickwick Papers* in 1836. The Great Exhibition was held in 1851.

CAREER

1831	Entered Middle Temple, but soon left.
1833	Bought *The National Standard & Journal of Literature, Science, Music, Theatricals and the Fine Arts*, a struggling weekly, which failed.
1834–7	In Paris studying drawing.
1836	Published *Floreat Zephyr* (satirical drawings). Became Paris correspondent of the *Constitutional*.
1836	Married. Published *Flore et Zephyr*, his first work to be published in volume form.
1837	Returned to England and wrote for *The Times* and *Fraser's Magazine*.
1840	Separated from his wife on the grounds of her insanity. Published *The Paris Sketch Book*.
1841	Published *Comic Tales and Sketches*.

1841	Published *The History of Samuel Titmarsh*, under the pseudonym Michael Angelo Titmarsh, and *The Great Hoggarty Diamond*.
1842	Toured Ireland.
1842–6	Contributed to *Punch*.
1843	Published *The Irish Sketch Book*.
1844	Published *The Luck of Barry Lyndon*.
1846	Published *Cornhill to Cairo*.
1846–50	Published a yearly *Christmas Book*.
1848	Published *Vanity Fair*, with illustrations by the author, which was a tremendous success.

> A woman with fair opportunities and without a positive hump, may marry whom she likes.
>
> *Vanity Fair*, ch. 4

> Whenever he met a great man he grovelled before him, and my-lorded him as only a free-born Briton can do.
>
> Ibid., ch. 13.

> I think I could be a good woman if I had five thousand a year.
>
> Ibid., ch. 36

1848–50	Published *The History of Pendennis*.

> Remember, it is as easy to marry a rich woman as a poor woman.
>
> *The History of Pendennis*, ch. 28.

1851	Published his *Ode to May* on the Great Exhibition.

> These, England's triumphs, are the trophies of a bloodless war.
>
> *Ode to May*

1851–3	Lecturing in America.

1852	Published *The History of Henry Esmond* and lectured in America.

> 'Tis not the dying for a faith that's so hard, Master Harry – every man of every nation has done that – 'tis the living up to it that is difficult.
>
> *The History of Henry Esmond*, bk 1, ch. 6
>
> 'Tis strange what a man may do, and a woman yet think him an angel.
>
> Ibid., bk 1, ch. 7

1852	Published *The Newcomers*.
1855–6	Lecturing in America.
1857	Published *The Virginians*, which was set partly in America.
1860–2	First editor of the *Cornhill Magazine*.
DEATH	On Christmas Eve, 1863, suddenly, aged 52. Buried in Westminster Abbey.
HOBBIES & INTERESTS	Art and drawing; he illustrated several of his books.

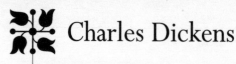

Charles Dickens

Prolific writer of immense popular and critical appeal, who achieved sudden fame with Pickwick Papers. *His novels, which described contemporary poverty, were all, except for* A Christmas Carol, *published in weekly or monthly instalments.*

BIRTH	1812, at 393 Old Commercial Road, Portsmouth, son of a Navy pay clerk.
MARITAL	Married, 1836, Catherine Hogarth. Separated 1858. Seven sons and three daughters.
EDUCATION	William Giles School, Chatham, and Wellington House Academy, London.

 A Little Bit of Background

The Stockton and Darlington Railway opened in 1825. The Reform Act, which extended the electorate and reformed Parliament, was passed in 1832. Europe was wracked by revolution in 1848. The Crimean War ended in 1856. Anthony Trollope's *The Warden* was published in 1855. The American Civil War ended in 1865.

CAREER	
1824	Worked in a shoe-blacking factory (his father being in prison for debt).
	Worked in an office making up parcels.
	Reported House of Commons debates for the *True Sun* (later the *Morning Chronicle*).
1833–5	Contributed to *The Monthly Magazine*.
1835	Contributed to *The Evening Chronicle*.
1836	His collected articles published as *Sketches by Boz*.
	Married.
	Began *The Posthumous Papers of the Pickwick Club*.

I wants to make your flesh creep.

The Fat Boy, *Pickwick Papers*, ch. 8, 1837

'It's always best on these occasions to do what the mob do.'
'But suppose there are two mobs?' suggested Mr Snodgrass.
'Shout with the largest,' replied Mr Pickwick.

Ibid., ch. 13

1837–9   *Oliver Twist* published in *Bentley's Miscellany.*

'Please, sir, I want some more.'

Oliver Twist, ch. 2

'If the law supposes that,' said Mr Bumble . . .
'the law is a ass – a idiot.'

Ibid., ch. 51

1838–9   *Nicholas Nickleby* published in monthly instalments.

He had but one eye, and the popular prejudice
runs in favour of two.

Nicholas Nickleby, ch. 4

I pity his ignorance and despise him.

Fanny Squeers, *Nicholas Nickleby*, ch. 15

1840–1   *The Old Curiosity Shop* and *Barnaby Rudge* published.
1842   Went to America, where he promoted the idea of
international copyright and attacked the idea of slavery.
1843   Wrote *A Christmas Carol.*

'Bah', said Scrooge. 'Humbug!'

A Christmas Carol, stave 1

1843–4   *Martin Chuzzlewit* published.

Affection beaming in one eye, and calculation shining out of the other.

Mrs Todgers, *Martin Chuzzlewit*, ch. 8

'Here's the rule for bargains: "Do other men, for they would do you." That's the true business precept.'

Jonas Chuzzlewit, ibid., ch. 11

'He'd make a lovely corpse.'

Mrs Gamp, ibid., ch. 25

1844	Lived in Genoa, where he wrote *The Chimes*.
1846	Editor of *The Daily News*.
	Went to Switzerland, where he wrote *Dombey and Son* and *The Battle of Life*.
1847	Manager of a travelling theatrical company.
1848	Published *The Haunted Man*.
1849–50	Published *David Copperfield* in monthly instalments

'Annual income twenty pounds, annual expenditure nineteen nineteen six, result happiness. Annual income twenty pounds, annual expenditure twenty pounds nought and six, result misery.'

Mr Micawber, *David Copperfield*, ch. 12

'We are so very 'umble.'

Uriah Heep, ibid., ch. 17

'It was as true . . . as taxes is. And nothing's truer than them.'

Mr Barkis, ibid., ch. 21

'What a world of gammon and spinnage it is, though, ain't it!'

Miss Mowcher, ibid., ch. 22

| 1850 | Founded the journals *Household Words* and *All the Year Round*. |
| 1852–3 | Published *Bleak House*. |

> 'This is a London particular . . . A fog, miss.'
>
> *Bleak House*, ch. 3
>
> The one great principle of the English law is, to make business for itself.
>
> Ibid., ch. 39

| 1854 | Published *Hard Times*. |

> 'Now, what I want is, Facts . . . Facts alone are wanted in life.'
>
> Mr Gradgrind, *Hard Times*, bk 1, ch. 1

1855–7	Published *Little Dorritt*.
1858	Separated from his wife.
	Started his public readings.
1859	Published *A Tale of Two Cities*.

> It was the best of times, it was the worst of times, it was the age of wisdom, it was the age of foolishness, it was the epoch of belief, it was the epoch of incredulity, it was the season of Light, it was the season of Darkness, it was the spring of hope, it was the winter of despair, we had everything before us, we had nothing before us, we were all going direct to Heaven, we were all going direct the other way.
>
> *A Tale of Two Cities*, bk 1, ch. 1
>
> It is a far, far better thing that I do, than I have ever done; it is a far, far better rest that I go to, than I have ever known.
>
> Sydney Carton's thoughts on the scaffold, ibid., bk 3, ch. 15

| 1860–1 | Published *Great Expectations*. |

> It is a most miserable thing to feel ashamed of home.
>
> *Great Expectations*, ch. 14

1864–5	Published *Our Mutual Friend*.

> 'I think . . . that it is the best club in London.'
>
> Mr Twemlow, on the House of Commons, *Our Mutual Friend*, bk 2, ch. 3
>
> 'He'd be sharper than a serpent's tooth, if he wasn't as dull as ditch water.'
>
> Fanny Cleaver, ibid., bk 3, ch. 10

1867/8	Gave public readings in America.
1870	Began *The Mystery of Edwin Drood*.
DEATH	1870, aged 58, leaving it for ever a mystery why Edwin Drood disappeared. Buried in Westminster Abbey.
HOBBIES & INTERESTS	The occult.

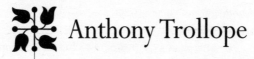 # Anthony Trollope

Novelist who also had a successful career in the Post Office,
author of 47 novels, including the Barsetshire and Palliser
series, which established the tradition of 'novel sequence' in
English fiction. He also invented the pillar box.

BIRTH	1815, in Bloomsbury, London.
MARITAL STATUS	Married, 1844, Rose Heseltine, of Rotherham. Two sons.
EDUCATION	Harrow and Winchester.

 ## A Little Bit of Background

The Penny Post was introduced in 1840. Thackeray published *Vanity Fair* in 1847. Lord Palmerston was Prime Minister between 1859 and 1865. Civil Service exams were introduced in 1870.

CAREER

1834	Post Office clerk.
1841	Post Office surveyor in Ireland.
1847	Post Office Inspector of Deliveries, south-west rural Ireland. Published his first novel, *The Macdermots of Ballycloran*.
1855–67	Published *The Warden*, followed by *Barchester Towers* (1857) and then the four remaining novels in the Barsetshire series. He regarded *The Last Chronicle* (1867) as his best novel.

The end of a novel, like the end of a children's dinner-party, must
be made up of sweetmeats and sugar-plums.

Barchester Towers, ch. 53

1858	Visited Egypt and the West Indies.
1859	Promoted to supervisor of Eastern Postal District.

1859	Introduced the pillar box, his own invention.
1862	Visited America.
1866	Retired from the Post Office.

> 'It's dogged as does it. It ain't thinking about it.'
>
> Giles Hoggett, *The Last Chronicles of Barset*, ch. 61, 1867

1867–80	Edited the *St Paul's Magazine*.
1868	Stood unsuccessfully as a Liberal MP.
1869	Began a series of political novels, the first being *Phineas Finn*.
1871–2	Visited Australia and New Zealand.

> We cannot have heroes to dine with us. There are none. And were those heroes to be had, we should not like them . . . the persons whom you cannot care for in a novel, because they are so bad, are the very same that you so dearly love in your life, because they are so good.
>
> *The Eustace Diamonds*, ch. 35, 1873

1878	Visited South Africa.

> A novel can hardly be made interesting or successful without love . . . It is necessary because the passion is one which interests or has interested all. Everyone feels it, has felt it, or expects to feel it.
>
> *Autobiography*, ch. 12, 1883

> Three hours a day will produce as much as a man ought to write.
>
> Ibid., ch. 15

DEATH	1882, aged 67, in London. Buried at Kensal Green Cemetery.
HOBBIES & INTERESTS	Hunting.

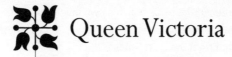 # Queen Victoria

Queen of the United Kingdom of Great Britain and Ireland, 1837–1901, and Empress of India from 1876, who gave her name to an age and presided over the industrialisation of her nation.

BIRTH	1819, at Kensington Palace, only child of Edward, Duke of Kent, fourth son of George III, d. 1820, and Victoria of Saxe-Coburg.
MARITAL STATUS	Married, 1840, Albert of Saxe-Coburg & Gotha, d. 1861. Four sons and five daughters.
EDUCATION	Tutored by Fraulein Louise Lehzen, 1820–7, and by the Revd George Davys, 1827–37.

 ## A Little Bit of Background

British colonists arrived in New Zealand in 1840. 1846 saw the repeal of the Corn Laws, the attempt to ensure a sufficient home-grown supply by regulating imports and exports. The Great Exhibition occurred in 1851. The Indian Mutiny took place 1857–8. Charles Barry's Houses of Parliament opened in 1860. In 1867, Canada was established as the First Dominion. Gordon was killed at Khartoum in 1885.

> 'I will be good.'
>
> On being shown a chart of the line of succession, 11 March 1830,
> *The Prince Consort*, Theodore Martin, vol. 1, ch. 2, 1875

CAREER	
1838	Crowned.

> 'It was with some emotion . . . that I beheld Albert – who is beautiful.'
>
> Of her first meeting with Prince Albert, *c.* 1838, attributed,
> *Albert: Uncrowned King*, Stanley Weintraub, 1997

1840	Married.
1840	First assassination attempt by Edward Oxford, an insane potboy.
	Gave birth to her first child, a girl.
1842	Second child, a boy (the future Edward VII).
	Her first railway journey (Slough to Paddington).
	Second assassination attempt.
	Third assassination attempt.
1843	Third child, a girl.
	First trip abroad, to France, the first time an English sovereign had visited a French sovereign since Henry VIII attended the Field of the Cloth of Gold in 1520.
1845	Visited Germany for the first time.
1846	Fourth child, a girl.
1850	Fifth child, a boy.
1851	Osborne, Isle of Wight, completed.
1854	Balmoral Castle completed.
1854–6	Crimean War.
1856	Instituted the Victoria Cross for 'acts of conspicuous valour in war'.
1857	Indian Mutiny.
1861	Prince Albert died suddenly, from typhoid.
1868	First visit to Switzerland.
1870	Signed orders agreeing to Army reforms.

The Queen is most anxious to enlist every one who can speak or write to join in checking this mad, wicked folly of Woman's Rights, with all its attendant horrors, on which her poor feeble sex is bent, forgetting every sense of womanly feeling and propriety.

1876	Made Empress of India.
1879	First visit to Italy.

'He speaks to Me as if I was a public meeting.'
Of Gladstone, *Collections and Recollections*, G.W.E. Russell, ch. 14, 1898

1882	Fifth assassination attempt.
1887	Golden Jubilee.

1889	First visit to Spain by an English sovereign. Entertained her grandson, the German Emperor. He made her colonel of his 1st Regiment of Horse Guards.

The danger to the country, to Europe, to her vast Empire, which is involved in having all these great interests entrusted to the shaking hand of an old, wild, and incomprehensible man of 82, is very great!

On Gladstone's last appointment as Prime Minister, letter to Lord Lansdowne, 12 August 1892, *Lord Lansdowne*, T. Wodehouse Legh, 1929

1897	Diamond Jubilee.

The future Vice Roy must . . . not be guided by the snobbish and vulgar, over-bearing and offensive behaviour of our Civil and Political Agents, if we are to go on peaceably and happily in India . . . not trying to trample on the people and continuously reminding them and making them feel they are a conquered people.

Letter to Lord Salisbury, 27 May 1898, *Superior Person*, Kenneth Rose, ch. 23, 1969

'We are not interested in the possibilities of defeat; they do not exist.'

On the Boer War during 'Black Week', following three major defeats, December 1899, *Life of Robert, Marquis of Salisbury*, Lady Gwendolen Cecil, vol. 3, ch. 6, 1931

'We are not amused.'

Attributed, 2 January 1900, *Notebooks of a Spinster Lady*, Caroline Holland, ch. 21, 1919

DEATH	1901, aged 81, at Osborne, Isle of Wight. Buried at Frogmore Mausoleum, Windsor Castle.
HOBBIES & INTERESTS	Scotland and India.

Florence Nightingale

Englishwoman, known as the Lady of the Lamp, who raised nursing from a disreputable profession to the status of an honoured vocation.

BIRTH	1820, in Florence, Italy.
MARITAL STATUS	Single.
EDUCATION	At home.

 ## A Little Bit of Background

Elizabeth Fry, the prison reformer, founded an order of nurses in 1833. The Crimean War took place in 1854–6, the American Civil War in 1861–5. The International Red Cross was founded in Switzerland in 1864. The Franco–Prussian War occurred in 1870.

CAREER

1844–55	Visited hospitals in London and abroad.
1849–50	Toured Egypt.
1851	Trained as 'sicknurse' at the Kaiserwerth Institute for Deaconesses and Nurses.
1853	Superintendent of Hospital for Invalid Gentlewomen in Chandos Street, London.
1854	Appointed 'Lady-in-Chief' at Scutari Barrack Hospital, Crimea.
	Known by soldiers as 'the lady with the lamp'.
	Made vast improvements to the insanitary kitchens and laundry, and introduced provision for the soldiers' wives and children.
1855	Visited Balaclava hospitals and caught a fever. Introduced reading and recreation rooms.
1856	Invited to visit Queen Victoria.

1857	Published notes on *Hospital Administration for the British Army*.
1860	Nightingale School and Home for Nurses established at St Thomas' Hospital, London.

> I would earnestly ask my sisters to keep clear of both the jargons now current everywhere . . . of the jargon, namely about the 'rights' of women, which urges women to do all that men do . . . merely because men do it, and without regard to whether this is the best that women can do; and of the jargon which urges women to do nothing that men do, merely because they are women . . . Woman should bring the best she has, whatever that is . . . without attending to either of these cries.
>
> *Notes on Nursing*, 1860

> No man, not even a doctor, ever gives any other definition of what a nurse should be than this – 'devoted and obedient'. This definition would do just as well for a porter. It might even do for a horse. It would not do for a policeman.
>
> Ibid.

1862–4	Consulted by both sides in American Civil War.

> It may seem a strange principle to enunciate as the very first requirement in a Hospital that it should do the sick no harm.
>
> *Notes on Hospitals*, Preface, 1863 ed.

1862	Helped found nursing home in Liverpool Infirmary.
1868	Helped found East London Nursing Society.
1870–1	Consulted by both sides in the Franco–German War.
1874	Helped found the Workhouse Nursing Association.
1890	Helped found the Queen's Jubilee Nursing Institute.
1907	Awarded the Order of Merit.

> 'Too kind, too kind.'
>
> On the Order of Merit being brought to her at her home,
> 5 December 1907, *Life of Florence Nightingale*,
> E. Cook, vol. 2, pt 7, ch. 9, 1913

1908 Given Freedom of City of London.

DEATH 1910, aged 90, in London. Her family declined the offer of burial at Westminster Abbey and she was instead buried in East Wellow church.

HOBBIES & INTERESTS Egypt.

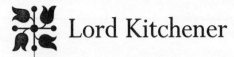

Lord Kitchener

Horatio Herbert Kitchener, First Earl Kitchener of Khartoum and Broome, and British First World War Field Marshal, who oversaw the voluntary enlistment of over three million men.

BIRTH	1850, in County Kerry, Ireland.
MARITAL STATUS	Single. In 1884, he became engaged to Hermione Baker, who died of typhoid in Cairo.
EDUCATION	Royal Military Academy, Woolwich.

 ## A Little Bit of Background

Dr Gatling invented his machine gun in 1862, and in 1866 Alfred Nobel invented dynamite. 1882 saw the occupation of Egypt, and 1896 the conquest of Sudan. The Second Boer War took place 1899–1902. The Delhi Durbar was held in 1911. The First World War or Great War lasted from 1914 to 1918.

CAREER	
1871	Commission in Royal Engineers.
1874	Seconded to Palestine Exploration Fund.
1878	Surveying Cyprus.
1882	Second-in-Command of Egyptian Cavalry.
1884–5	In Wolseley's failed expedition to relieve General Gordon at Khartoum.
1886	Governor-General of Eastern Sudan.
1888	Adjutant-General of Egyptian Army.
1889	Involved in the defeat of the Dervishes at Toski. CB (Companion of the Order of the Bath).
1892	Sirdar of Egyptian Army.
1892–6	Put army in readiness for the conquest of Sudan.
1894	KCMG.

1896	Promoted to Major General and KCB for River War.
1898	Destroyed the Khalifa's (Mahdi's) army at Omdurman and reoccupied Khartoum.
1898	Dealt tactfully with the French at Fashoda on the White Nile.
1899	Governor General of Sudan.
	Chief of Lord Roberts' staff in South Africa.
1900–2	Subdued the Cape Boer rebellion in the Priska region and pacified the south of the Orange Free State.
1902	Created Viscount. OM.
1902–9	Commander-in-Chief in India.
	Abolished dual military control so that the Indian Army no longer received orders from both London and Delhi.
	Established Indian Staff College.
1909	Field Marshal.
1911	Consul General in Egypt.
1914	Created Earl. Secretary of State for War.

You are ordered abroad as a soldier of the King to help our French comrades against the invasion of a common enemy . . . In this new experience you may find temptations both in wine and women. You must entirely resist both temptations, and, while treating all women with perfect courtesy, you should avoid any intimacy. Do your duty bravely. Fear God. Honour the King.

Message to soldiers of the British Expeditionary Force,
The Times, 19 August 1914

'I don't mind your being killed, but I object to your being taken prisoner.'

To the Prince of Wales, 18 December 1914,
Journals and Letters of Reginald Viscount Esher, vol. 3, 1938

1914–16	Expanded the British Army from six regular and fourteen territorial divisions to 70 divisions – 3 million men having volunteered.

> Your country needs YOU!
>
> Recruitment poster

1915 | KG (Knight of the Order of the Garter).

DEATH | 1916, aged 65. Died when HMS *Hampshire*, which was taking him to Russia, struck a mine off the Orkney Islands.

HOBBIES & INTERESTS | Jigsaw puzzles.

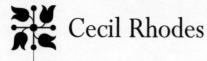

Cecil Rhodes

English-born South African statesman and financier, Prime Minister of the Cape Colony 1890–6, who helped found Rhodesia.

BIRTH	1853, in Bishop's Stortford, Hertfordshire, the fifth son of a vicar.
MARITAL STATUS	Single.
EDUCATION	Bishop's Stortford Grammar School and Oriel College, Oxford (he matriculated in 1873 and eventually graduated in 1881).

 ### A Little Bit of Background

In 1836, the Boers made the Great Trek. 1879 saw the Zulu War and 1880 the First Boer War. The Jameson Raid, the invasion of the Transvaal from Mafeking, took place in December 1895. 1896 saw the conquest of Sudan, and 1899–1902 the Second Boer War.

CAREER

1870   Owing to weak health, sent to Natal to help his eldest brother farm cotton.

> The real fact is that I could no longer stand their eternal cold mutton.
>
> Explaining why he left home, *Cecil Rhodes*, Gordon le Sueur, 1913

1871   Went to the Orange Free State in search of diamonds.
Bought into the Kimberley diamond field and acquired a large interest in De Beers mines.

1875   Travelled through Bechuanaland and Transvaal.

1880–1902   Elected to Cape legislature.

1880	Helped establish De Beers Mining Company.
1884	Deputy Commissioner (when Bechuanaland was formally annexed).
1887–8	Became Chairman of De Beers Consolidated Mines and acquired a significant stake in Consolidated Goldfields.
1889	Agreed terms with Lobengula, king of Matabeleland, allowing the newly incorporated British South Africa Company to administer territory north of Bechuana – renamed Rhodesia.
1893–4	Directed the war with the Matabeles.
1890–6	Prime Minister of the Cape.

'How can I possibly dislike a sex to which Your Majesty belongs?'

In response to Queen Victoria's suggestion he did not like women, *Rhodes*, Lockhart

1899–1900	Besieged in Kimberley.
1901–02	Travelling in Europe.

Ask any man what nationality he would prefer to be, and ninety-nine out of a hundred will tell you that they would prefer to be Englishmen.

Cecil Rhodes, Gordon le Sueur, 1913

Remember that you are an Englishman and have consequently won first prize in the lottery of life.

Dear Me, Peter Ustinov, ch. 4

DEATH	1902, aged 49, at Muizenberg in South Africa. Buried at Matopos Hills, near Bulawayo, Zimbabwe. His will endowed 170 scholarships at Oxford for students from the colonies, the US and Germany. He also left £100,000 to Oriel College.

'So little done, so much to do.'

His last words

HOBBIES & INTERESTS	Precious stones.

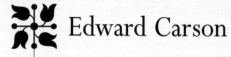

Edward Carson

Edward Henry Carson, later Baron Carson. Brilliant Irish lawyer and MP, who led the Irish Unionists in the House of Commons in their opposition to Home Rule. His legal reputation was made through his cross-examination of Oscar Wilde during the latter's celebrated libel action against the Marquess of Queensberry.

BIRTH	1854, in Dublin.
MARITAL STATUS	Married first, 1879, Sarah Foster, d. 1913. Two sons and two daughters. Secondly, 1914, Ruby Frewen. One son.
EDUCATION	Portarlington School and Trinity College, Dublin.

A Little Bit of Background

The Home Rule Act, granting Ireland an independent Parliament, was passed in 1914. The Easter Rising took place in Dublin in 1916, and the Anglo-Irish War between 1919 and 1920. In 1919, six of the nine counties of Ulster elected for partition from the new Irish Free State, and the Anglo-Irish Treaty, allowing for the partition of Ireland, was signed in December 1921. 1922–3 saw the Irish Civil War.

CAREER

1877	Called to the Irish Bar.
1887	Junior Counsel to Attorney-General.
1889	Queen's Counsel (QC).
1892	Solicitor General for Ireland.
1892–1918	MP for Dublin University.
1893	Called to the English Bar.
1895	His genius as an advocate displayed in Oscar Wilde's libel action against Lord Queensberry.
1900–5	Solicitor General for England.

1900	Knighted.
1905	Privy Councillor (PC).
1910	Leader of Irish Unionists in the House of Commons.
1911	Leader of the movement for provisional government of Ulster.

> 'I now enter into compact with you, and with the help of God you and I joined together . . . will yet defeat the most nefarious conspiracy that has ever been hatched against a free people . . . We must be prepared . . . the morning Home Rule passes, ourselves to become responsible for the government of the Protestant Province of Ulster.'
>
> Speech at Craigavon, 23 September 1911

1912	Raised Ulster Volunteer Force and drafted the Solemn League and Covenant.
1913	Advocated that the Province of Ulster be exempt from the Home Rule Bill.
	Widowed.

> 'My one affection left me is my love for Ireland.'
>
> Following the death of his wife, 1913, *Carson*, Montgomery Hyde, 1953

1915–16	Attorney General.
1916–17	First Lord of the Admiralty.

> From the day I first entered parliament up to the present, devotion to the union has been the guiding star of my political life.
>
> In *Dictionary of National Biography*, 1917
>
> My only great qualification for being put at the head of the Navy is that I am very much at sea.
>
> *Life of Lord Carson*, Ian Colvin, vol. 3, ch. 23, 1936

1918	Resigned over his opposition to the Home Rule Bill.
1918–21	MP for Duncairn, Belfast.

1921	Resigned as Leader of the Ulster Unionists.
1921–9	Lord of Appeal in Ordinary.
DEATH	1935, aged 81. He was accorded the only ever state funeral in Northern Ireland, and is buried in St Anne's Cathedral, Belfast.
HOBBIES & INTERESTS	The Law.

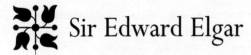

Sir Edward Elgar

Edward William Elgar, English composer, violinist and conductor who wrote the Enigma *Variations.*

BIRTH   1857 Lower Broadheath, near Worcester, son of an organist.

MARITAL STATUS   Married, 1889, Alice Roberts, d. 1920. One daughter.

EDUCATION   Left school at the age of 15.

CAREER
1873   Worked for a year for a local solicitor.
1874   Taught piano and violin.
1879   Band Master to Worcester and County Lunatic Asylum.
1885   Replaced his father as organist of St George's Church, Worcester.
1889   Following his marriage, he moved to London. His wife encouraged him to turn from the violin to composition.
1890   Completed the *Froissart* overture.
1896   Wrote *The Light of Life* and *Scenes from the Saga of King Olaf.*

> If I write you a tune, you say it is commonplace — if I don't you all say it is rot.
>
> Letter to A.J. Jaegar, 1898

1899   *Enigma Variations.*

> To my friends pictured within.
>
> Dedication, *Enigma Variations*, 1899

> I essay much, I hope little, I ask nothing.
>
> Inscription at the end of *Enigma Variations*, 1899

1900   *The Dream of Gerontius.*

> Lovely day: Sun-Zephyr-view-window open-liver-pills-proofs-bills-weedkiller-yah!
>
> Letter to A.J. Jaegar

1901–7	*Pomp and Circumstance* marches.
1901	Overture *Cockaigne*.
1902–14	Four visits to America.
1903	*The Apostles*.
1904	Knighted.
1905	*Introduction and Allegro for Strings*.
1905–8	Professor of Music at Birmingham University.
1906	*The Kingdom*.
1908	*Symphony in A Flat*.
1910	*Violin Concerto*.
1911	*Symphony in E Flat*.
	Order of Merit (OM).
1913	*Falstaff*.
1919	*Violoncello Concerto*.
1920	Wife died.
1924	Master of the King's Music.
1928	KCVO.
1931	Created Baronet.

> 'There is music in the air.'
>
> *Sir Edward Elgar*, R.J. Buckley, ch. 4, 1905

DEATH	1934, aged 76. Buried next to his wife at St Wulfstan's Church, Little Malvern, Worcestershire.
HOBBIES & INTERESTS	The violin and bicycling.

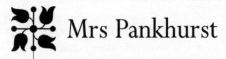 # Mrs Pankhurst

English suffragette leader often imprisoned for damaging property, but who abandoned her campaign for the duration of the First World War.

BIRTH | 1858, as Emmeline Goulden, in Manchester.

MARITAL STATUS | Married, 1879, R.M. Pankurst, d. 1898. Three daughters, including Christabel and Sylvia, and one son.

EDUCATION | Privately.

 ## A Little Bit of Background

The Labour Party was founded in 1900. In 1918, men aged 21 and over and women aged 30 and over received the vote. Women aged 21 and over got the vote in 1929.

CAREER

1879 | Married R.M. Pankhurst, a Manchester barrister.
1898 | Widowed.
1903 | Founded Women's Social and Political Union with her eldest daughter, Christabel Pankhurst.
1905 | Became increasingly militant.

> The argument of the broken window pane is the most valuable argument in modern politics.
>
> *The Strange Death of Liberal England,*
> George Dangerfield, pt. 2, ch. 3, 1936

1908 | Imprisoned in Holloway Gaol.
1909/11/13 | Visited US.
1912 | For two years she was repeatedly arrested, went on hunger strike and released.

'There is something that Governments care far more for than human life, and that is the security of property, and so it is through property that we shall strike the enemy . . . I say to the Government: You have not dared to take the leaders of Ulster for their incitement to rebellion. Take me if you dare.'

Speech at the Albert Hall, 17 October 1912, *My Own Story*, Emmeline Pankhurst, 1914

1914	At the outbreak of war, abandoned her campaign and encouraged women to do industrial war work.
1918	Achieved women's suffrage for those aged 30 and over. (Women aged 21 and over received the vote in 1929).
DEATH	1928, aged 70. Buried at Brompton Cemetery, London.
HOBBIES & INTERESTS	Democracy.

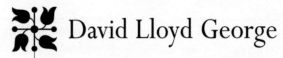
David Lloyd George

British Liberal statesman who, as Chancellor, introduced the People's Budget in 1909 and, as Prime Minister, 1916–22, led Britain through the latter half of the First World War.

BIRTH | 1863 in Manchester. Bought up in Llanystumdwy, Gwynedd, by his widowed mother and his uncle, a cobbler.

MARITAL STATUS | Married first, 1888, Margaret Owen. Two sons and three daughters. Secondly, 1943, Frances Stevenson (his personal secretary). One daughter.

EDUCATION | Llanystumdwy village school.

 ## A Little Bit of Background

The House of Lords veto for finance bills was abolished in 1911. The First World War, or Great War, took place 1914–18, the Anglo-Irish War in 1919–20 and the Second World War 1939–45.

CAREER

1884 | Qualified as a solicitor.

1890 | Elected Liberal MP for Caernarfon Boroughs (a seat he retained until 1945). Championed Welsh causes. Opposed the Boer War.

1905 | President of the Board of Trade.

1908 | Chancellor of the Exchequer.

> 'I have no nest-eggs. I am looking for someone else's hen-roost to rob next year.'
>
> As Chancellor, 1908, *Tempestuous Journey*, Frank Owen, ch. 10, 1954

1909 | Delivered his 'People's Budget', which was designed to fund social services by taxing land, but it was rejected by the House of Lords, which exercised its veto.

'A fully-equipped duke costs as much to keep up as two Dreadnoughts [battleships]; and dukes are just as great a terror and they last longer.'

Speech, Newcastle, 9 October 1909, reported in *The Times*, 11 October 1909

1910	Liberals re-elected and the Budget passed.
1911	Introduced contributory schemes for Health and Unemployment Services.
	Accused of insider trading (in American shares in Marconi), but cleared 1912.
1914	Dealt with initial crisis of the First World War.

'The great peaks of honour we had forgotten – Duty, Patriotism, and – clad in glittering white – the great pinnacle of Sacrifice, pointing like a rugged finger to Heaven.'

Speech, Queen's Hall, London, 19 September 1914, reported in *The Times*, 20 September 1914

1914	First wartime Budget – doubled income tax.
1915	Secretary of State for War.
1916	Prime Minister of Coalition government.
1918	Returned at election with large Unionist majority but only 133 Liberal supporters.

'At eleven o'clock this morning came to an end the cruellest and most terrible war that has ever scourged mankind. I hope we may say that thus, this fateful morning, came to an end all wars.'

Speech, House of Commons, 11 November 1918

'What is our task? To make Britain a fit country for heroes to live in.'

Speech, Wolverhampton, 23 November 1918, reported in *The Times*, 25 November 1918

'Unless I am mistaken, by the steps we have taken [in Ireland] we have murder by the throat.'

Speech, Mansion House, London, 9 November 1920,
Tempestuous Journey, Frank Owen, ch. 28, 1954

'Negotiating with de Valera . . . is like trying to pick up mercury with a fork.'

To which de Valera replied, 'Why doesn't he use a spoon?',
Eamon de Valera, M.J. MacManus, ch. 6, 1944

1922	Accused of selling peerages and other honours to fund his own political aims.
1931	Retired to his estate at Churt.
1932	Published *The Truth about Reparations and War Debts*.
1933	Published *War Memoirs*.
1936	Visited Hitler.
1938	Published *The Truth about the Peace Treaties*.
1940	Created Earl of Dwyfor.
DEATH	1945, aged 82. Buried in Llanystumdwy, on the bank of the River Dwyfor.
HOBBIES & INTERESTS	Cars and golf.

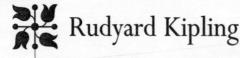

Rudyard Kipling

Rudyard Joseph Kipling, journalist and writer, author of
The Jungle Book *and* Kim, *and the poem* If; *the*
'unofficial poet laureate of the Empire'.

BIRTH	1865, in Bombay, India. His father was the Principal of the School of Art, Lahore. His mother was the sister-in-law of Edward Burne-Jones.
MARITAL STATUS	Married, 1892, Caroline Balestier, the sister of his American agent. One son and one daughter, both of whom predeceased him.
EDUCATION	United Services College, Westward Ho!

 ## A Little Bit of Background

1877 saw the Proclamation of the Empire of India, 1899–1902 the Second Boer War and 1914–18 the First World War.

CAREER

1882	Reporter for the *Lahore Civil and Military Gazette*.
1886	Published *Departmental Ditties*.
1888	Published *Plain Tales from the Hills* and *Soldiers Three*.
1889	Moved to London.
1890	Published *Wee Willie Winkie*.
1891	Published *The Light That Failed*.
1892	Married Caroline Balestier.
1892–6	Lived in Brattleboro, Vermont, USA.
1892	Published *Barrack-Room Ballads*.

Oh, East is East, and West is West, and never the twain shall meet,
Till Earth and Sky stand presently at God's great Judgement Seat;
But there is neither East nor West, Border, nor Breed, nor birth,
When two strong men stand face to face, tho' they come from the
ends of earth!   *The Ballad of East and West*, 1892

And what should they know of England who only England know?

The English Flag, 1892

Then it's Tommy this, an' Tommy that, an' 'Tommy 'ow's yer
soul?'
But it's 'Thin red line of 'eroes' when the drums begin to roll.

Tommy, 1892

1893	Published *Many Inventions*.
1894/5	Published *The Jungle Book*.
1896	Published *The Seven Seas*.
1897	Published *Captains Courageous* and *Recessional*.

Lord God of Hosts, be with us yet,
Lest we forget – lest we forget!

Recessional, 1897

1900	Visited South Africa.
1901	Published *Kim*.
1902	Moved to Burwash. Published the *Just So Stories*.

He walked by himself, and all places were alike to him.

The Cat that Walked by Himself, *Just So Stories*

One Elephant – a new Elephant – an Elephant's Child – who was
full of 'satiable curiosity.   The Elephant's Child, ibid.

1906	Published *Puck of Pook's Hill*.
1907	Won the Nobel Prize for Literature, the first English writer to do so.
1910	Published *Rewards and Fairies* and *If*.

If you can fill the unforgiving minute
With sixty seconds' worth of distance run,
Yours is the Earth and everything that's in it,
And – which is more – you'll be a Man, my son!

If

1911	Published *A School History of England*.
1916	His son killed in action in the First World War.

'Have you news of my boy Jack?'
Not this tide.
'When d'you think that he'll come back?
Not with this wind blowing, and this tide.

My Boy Jack, 1916, written after the death of his own son

My son was killed while laughing at some jest. I would I knew
What is was, and it might serve me in a time when jests are few.

Epitaphs of the War: A Son, 1919

1919	Adviser to the Imperial War Graves Commission.

A soldier of the Great War, Known unto God.

Words chosen by Kipling to be inscribed on the headstones of unknown soldiers

1937	Refused the Order of Merit three times.

My Daemon was with me in the *Jungle Books*, *Kim*, and both
Puck books, and good care I took to walk delicately lest he should
withdraw. I know that he did not, because when these books were
finished they said so themselves with, almost, the water-hammer
click of a tap turned off.

Something of Myself

	Fragment of his autobiography, *Something of Myself*, published posthumously.
DEATH	1936, aged 70, of a brain haemorrhage. Buried in Westminster Abbey.
HOBBIES & INTERESTS	India and France.

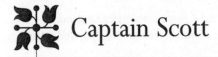 # Captain Scott

Robert Falcon Scott, English Antarctic explorer whose last, doomed, expedition inspired the nation.

BIRTH	1868, in Devonport.
MARITAL STATUS	Married, 1908, Kathleen Bruce, the sculptress (her statue of her husband stands at Waterloo Place, London). One son, the artist and ornithologist Sir Peter Scott.
EDUCATION	Joined the Navy at the age of 12.

 ## A Little Bit of Background

The Wright Brothers achieved the first manned powered flight in 1903. Sigmund Freud wrote the *Psychopathology of Everyday Life* in 1904. In 1905, Einstein published his theory of Relativity. Charlie Chaplin made his first film in 1913.

CAREER	
1880	Joined the Royal Navy.
1901–4	Led Antarctic expedition in the *Discovery* to survey, sound and record.
	Discovered Edward VII Land.
1910	Led second Antarctic expedition in the *Terra Nova*.
1912	Reached the Pole on 18 Jan 1912, a month after the Norwegian expedition led by Roald Amundsen. Lack of food and cold led to the death of the entire party some time after 29 March. Their diaries and bodies were discovered eight months later.

> Great God! This is an awful place.
>
> Diary, 17 January 1912, *Scott's Last Expedition*, vol. 1, ch. 18, 1913

> 'I am just going outside and may be some time.'
>
> Quoting the last words of Captain Oates, 'that very gallant gentleman', before he left the tent
> and disappeared into a snow storm, diary 17 March 1912

> Make the boy interested in natural history if you can; it is better
> than games.
>
> Last letter to his wife, ibid., vol. 1, ch. 20

> Had we lived, I should have had a tale to tell of the hardihood,
> endurance, and courage of my companions which would have
> stirred the heart of every Englishman. These rough notes and our
> dead bodies must tell the tale.
>
> 'Message to the Public' in late editions of *The Times*, 11 February 1913,
> and those of the following day, ibid., vol. 1, ch. 20

DEATH	1912, aged 44, on the return journey from the South Pole.
HOBBIES & INTERESTS	Natural history.

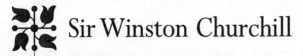

Sir Winston Churchill

Winston Leonard Spencer Churchill, British Prime Minister during the Second World War.

BIRTH	1874, at Blenheim Palace, son of Lord Randolph Churchill and Jennie Jerome, daughter of an American speculator, and grandson of the Duke of Marlborough.
MARITAL STATUS	Married, 1908, Clementine Hozier. One son, Randolph, and four daughters Diana, Sarah, Marigold and Mary.
EDUCATION	Harrow and Sandhurst. (Honorary degrees from more than 21 universities.)

 ## A Little Bit of Background

The Jameson Raid, the invasion of the Transvaal from Mafeking, took place in 1895. 1896 saw the conquest of Sudan, 1899–1902 the Boer War, and 1914–18 the First World War. The General Strike occurred in 1926. Edward VIII abdicated in 1936. The Second World War lasted from 1939 to 1945. Queen Elizabeth II succeeded to the throne in 1952.

CAREER	
1895	Commissioned in 4th Queen's Own Hussars.
	Action in Cuba with Spanish forces (which he reported for the *Daily Graphic*).
	Service on the North West Frontier, India.
1898	Published *The Story of the Malakand Field Force*.
	Participated in the last British cavalry charge at the Battle of Omdurman, Sudan.
1899	War Correspondent for *The Morning Post*. Sent to South Africa. Captured by the Boers and escaped.
1900	Published *London to Ladysmith, via Pretoria*.
	Published *Ian Hamilton's March*.
	Unionist MP for Oldham.

1904	Joined the Liberal Party.
1906	Published *Lord Randolph Churchill*.
	Liberal MP for North West Manchester.
1907	Privy Councillor (PC) and Parliamentary Under-Secretary for the Colonies.
1908	Published *My African Journey*.
	MP for Dundee. President of the Board of Trade.
	Married Clementine Hozier.

> NANCY ASTOR: If I were your wife I would put poison in your coffee!
>
> CHURCHILL: And if I were your husband I would drink it.
>
> *Glitter and Gold*, Consuelo Vanderbilt Balsan, 1952

1910	Home Secretary.
1911	Personally directed operations in the Sidney Street Siege, in which two armed anarchists died, an involvement for which he was much criticised.
1911–15	First Lord of the Admiralty, in which capacity he ensured that the Royal Navy was ready for the First World War.

> 'Naval tradition? Monstrous. Nothing but rum, sodomy, prayers, and the lash.'
>
> Often quoted as 'rum, sodomy and the lash', as in *Former Naval Person*, Peter Gretton, 1968, and *Diary*, Harold Nicolson, 17 August 1950

> 'Business carried on as usual during alterations on the map of Europe.'
>
> On the self-adopted 'motto' of the British people, speech, Guildhall, 9 November 1914, *Complete Speeches*, vol. 3, 1974

1915	Bonar Law demanded, and received, his resignation.
1916	Chancellor of the Duchy of Lancaster. Resigned and rejoined army.
	In command of 6th Battalion, Royal Scots Fusiliers, and served in France.

1917	Minister of Munitions.
1918	Coalition Liberal MP, Dundee.
1918–21	Secretary for War (and Air).
1921–2	Colonial Secretary.
1922	Defeated at Dundee. Bought his house, Chartwell.
1923	Published *World Crisis*.
1924–45	Conservative MP for Epping.

> 'Anyone can rat, but it takes a certain amount of ingenuity to re-rat.'
>
> On rejoining the Conservatives 20 years after leaving them for the Liberals, *c.* 1924

1924–9	Chancellor of the Exchequer.
1925	Returned Britain to the Gold Standard.
1926	Editor of *The British Gazette*.
1930	Published *My Early Life*.
1931	Resigned from shadow cabinet over India.
1936	Supported Edward VIII during the abdication crisis.
1937	Published *Great Contemporaries*.
1939	Returned to the Admiralty.

> Dictators ride to and fro upon tigers which they dare not dismount. And the tigers are getting hungry.
>
> Letter, 11 November 1937, quoted in *Step by Step*, 1939

> 'I cannot forecast to you the action of Russia. It is a riddle wrapped in a mystery inside an enigma.'
>
> Radio broadcast, 1 October 1939, quoted in *Into Battle*, 1941

1940–5	Prime Minister and Minister for Defence.

> 'I have nothing to offer but blood, toil, tears and sweat.'
>
> Speech, House of Commons, 13 May 1940

'What is our policy? . . .to wage war against a monstrous tyranny, never surpassed in the dark, lamentable catalogue of human crime.'

Ibid.

'What is our aim? . . . Victory, victory at all costs, victory in spite of all terror; victory, however long and hard the road may be; for without victory, there is no survival.'

Ibid.

'We shall not flag or fail. We shall go on to the end. We shall fight in France, we shall fight on the seas and oceans, we shall fight with growing confidence and growing strength in the air, we shall defend our island, whatever the cost may be. We shall fight on the beaches, we shall fight on the landing grounds, we shall fight in the fields and in the streets, we shall fight in the hills; we shall never surrender.'

Ibid., 4 June 1940

'Let us therefore brace ourselves to our duty, and so bear ourselves that, if the British Empire and its Commonwealth lasts for a thousand years, men will still say "This was their finest hour."'

Ibid., 18 June 1940

'Never in the field of human conflict was so much owed by so many to so few.'

On the Battle of Britain, ibid., 20 August 1940
('I thought he was talking about our mess bill' – British Spitfire pilot)

| **1941–65** | Lord Warden of the Cinque Ports. |

'Now this is not the end. It is not even the beginning of the end. But it is, perhaps, the end of the beginning.'

On the Battle of Egypt, speech at the Mansion House, London, 10 November 1942,
The End of the Beginning, 1943

'The empires of the future are the empires of the mind.'

> Speech at Harvard, 6 September 1942, *Complete Speeches*, vol. 7, 1974

| **1945–64** | MP for Woodford. |

'The Prime Minister has nothing to hide from the President of the United States.'

> On stepping from his bath in the presence of a startled President Roosevelt, recalled by Roosevelt's son in *Churchill*, a BBC TV series presented by Martin Gilbert, episode 3, 1992

'From Stettin in the Baltic to Trieste in the Adriatic an iron curtain has descended across the Continent.'

> Speech, Westminster College, Fulton, Missouri, 5 March 1946, *Complete Speeches*, vol. 7, 1974

'Democracy is the worst form of Government except all those other forms that have been tried from time to time.'

> Speech, House of Commons, 11 November 1947

| **1948** | Honorary Royal Academician Extraordinary. |
| **1948–54** | Published *The Second World War*. |

In war: resolution. In defeat: defiance. In victory: magnanimity. In peace: goodwill.

> Epigraph, which according to Edward Marsh in *A Number of People*, 1939, occurred to Churchill shortly after the conclusion of the First World War, *The Second World War*, vol. 1, 1948

1951–5	Prime Minister.
1953	Awarded the Nobel Prize for Literature.
	Knight of the Order of the Garter.

'I have accepted what many people have kindly said – namely, that I inspired the nation . . . It was the nation and the race dwelling all round the globe that had the lion's heart. I had the luck to be called upon to give the roar. I also hope that I sometimes suggested to the lion the right place to use his claws.'

> Speech, Westminster Hall, 30 November 1954

1956–8	Published *A History of the English-Speaking Peoples*.
DEATH	1965, aged 90. He lay in state in Westminster Hall and was then given a state funeral at St Paul's Cathedral. Buried in St Martin's Churchyard, Bladon.
HOBBIES & INTERESTS	Bricklaying, history, smoking, painting, pigs, food and drink.

'I have taken more out of alcohol than alcohol has taken out of me.'

By Quentin Reynolds, Quentin Reynolds, ch. 11, 1964

'Take away that pudding – it has no theme.'

The Way the Wind Blows, Lord Home , ch. 16, 1976

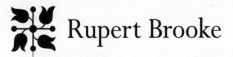 # Rupert Brooke

Rupert Chawner Brooke, soldier and First World War poet, whose work and death came to represent a generation.

BIRTH	1887, at 5 Hillmorton Road, Rugby, son of a Rugby School housemaster.
MARITAL STATUS	Single.
EDUCATION	Rugby and King's College, Cambridge (Scholar).

 ## A Little Bit of Background

Isaac Rosenberg and Wilfred Owen were other English poets who died during the First World War.

CAREER	
1909	First works published in journals. Travelled in Germany.
1911	Published *Poems 1911*.
1913	Became a fellow of King's College, Cambridge.
	Wrote a bleak, one-act play, *Lithuania*, after which he suffered a mental breakdown.
1913–14	As part of his recovery, visited America, Canada, New Zealand and the South Sea Islands, where he wrote 'Tiara Tahiti' and other poems, which some consider his best.
1914	Joined the RNVR (Royal Navy Volunteer Reserve).
1915	Took part in the Antwerp expedition.
	1914 and other poems published.
	Five 'War Sonnets', including 'If I should die', appeared in *New Numbers*.

> God! I will pack, and take a train,
> And get me to England once again!
> For England's the one land, I know,
> Where men with Splendid Hearts may go.
>
> *The Old Vicarage, Grantchester*, 1915

Rupert Brooke

Now, God be thanked Who has matched us with His hour,
And caught our youth, and wakened us from sleeping,
With hand made sure, clear eye, and sharpened power,
To turn, as swimmers into cleanness leaping.

Peace, 1914

If I should die, think only this of me:
That there's some corner of a foreign field
That is for ever England.

The Soldier, 1914

| **DEATH** | 1915, aged 28, of blood poisoning, on his way to the Dardanelles. Buried at Scyros, Greece. |
| **HOBBIES & INTERESTS** | Travel. |

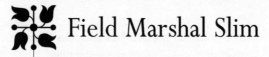

Field Marshal Slim

William Joseph Slim, later First Viscount Slim, Commander of the 'Forgotten Army' in Burma and India, led his troops to victory over the Japanese.

BIRTH	1891, near Bristol.
MARITAL STATUS	Married, 1926, Aileen Robertson. One son, one daughter.
EDUCATION	King Edward's School, Birmingham.

 ## A Little Bit of Background

The Second World War lasted from 1939 to 1945. The Japanese bombed Pearl Harbor in 1941 and took Singapore in 1942. In 1944, the Japanese were defeated at the Battle of Imphal. Atom bombs were dropped on Hiroshima and Nagasaki in 1945.

CAREER	
1914	Commissioned in the Royal Warwickshire Regiment.
1915–16	Serving in the Middle East. Awarded the MC.
1919	Transferred to the Indian Army.
1920	Joined 1/6th Gurkha Rifles.
1926–8	Staff College, Quetta.
1934	Indian Army Instructor, Staff College, Camberley.
1937	Commanded 2/7th Gurkhas.
1940	Commanded 10th Indian Infantry Brigade in Eritrea.
1941	Commanded 10th Indian Division in Iraq and Syria.
1942	Lieutenant General. Evacuated Burcorps from Burma. Made CBE (Commander of the British Empire).
1942–3	Arakan Campaign. Awarded the DSO (Distinguished Service Order).
1943	Commanded 14th Army.

| 1944 | Drive to Chindwin River, CB (Companion of the Order of the Bath), KCB (Knight Commander of the Bath). |
| 1945 | Took Meiketila and Mandalay. Recaptured Rangoon. Commander-in-Chief, Allied Land Forces, South-East Asia. |

'And then recall that exhilarating dash that carried you across the Irrawaddy . . . and there you met the Japanese Army in the open, and you tore it apart.'

Speech at Burma Reunion, quoted in *Quartered Safe Out Here*, George MacDonald Fraser

When you go home, tell them of us and say,
for your tomorrow we gave our today.

Kohima Memorial to the Burma Campaign

1946	GBE (Grand Cross of the British Empire).
1946–8	Commandant, Imperial Defence College.
1948	Chief of Imperial General Staff. Field Marshal.
1950	GCB (Grand Cross of the Bath).
1952	GCMG (Grand Cross of the Order of St Michael and St George).
1953–60	Governor General, Australia.
1954	GCVO (Grand Cross of the Royal Victorian Order).
1956	Published *Defeat into Victory*.
1957	Published *Courage and other Broadcasts*.
1959	Published *Unofficial History*.
1960	Created Viscount.
1964	Constable and Governor, Windsor Castle.
DEATH	1970, aged 79, in London.
HOBBIES & INTERESTS	Leadership.

George Orwell

Novelist and political essayist who challenged political opinion on both the right and the left.

BIRTH

1903, as Eric Arthur Blair, in Motihari, Bengal.

MARITAL STATUS

Married first, 1936, Eileen O'Shaughnessy, d. 1945. One adopted son. Secondly, 1949, shortly before he died, Sonia Brownwell.

EDUCATION

St Cyprian's Prep School (which he described in 'Such such were the joys' in so libellous a manner that the essay was not published in Britain until 1968) and Eton (Scholar):

Probably the battle of Waterloo was won on the playing-fields of Eton, but the opening battles of all subsequent wars have been lost there.

The Lion and the Unicorn, 'England, Your England', pt 1, 1941

 A Little Bit of Background

The Russian Revolution took place in 1917. Stalin came to power in 1924. The Spanish Civil War lasted from 1936 to 1939.

CAREER

1922–27

The Indian Imperial Police in Burma. Resigned in 1927:

to escape not only from Imperialism but every form of man's dominion over man.

Burmese Days, 1934

1928

Series of ill-paid jobs in Paris and London, described in *Down and out in Paris and London*, published in 1933.

1934	Published his first novel, *Burmese Days*.
1935	Published his second novel, *A Clergyman's Daughter*.
1936	Embarked on a journey to the North, which resulted in his commentary on working-class life, *The Road to Wigan Pier*, published in 1937.
	Published *Keep the Aspidistra Flying*, which he wrote whilst working in a Hampstead bookshop.
1936–7	Worked in a Hampshire bookshop.
1938	Fought for the Republican forces in the Spanish Civil War, an episode he described in *Homage to Catalonia*, published that year. Wounded and returned home.

Down here it was still the England I had known in my childhood: the railway cuttings smothered in wild flowers . . . the red buses, the blue policemen – all sleeping the deep, deep sleep of England, from which I sometimes fear that we shall never wake till we are jerked out of it by the roar of bombs.

Homage to Catalonia

1939	Published *Coming up for Air*.
1940–50	Published several collections of essays.

Old maids biking to Holy Communion through the mists of the autumn mornings . . . these are not only fragments, but characteristic fragments, of the English scene.

The Lion and the Unicorn, 'England, Your England', pt 1, 1941

1943–45	Literary editor of the socialist paper *The Tribune*.
1945	Published his first political satire, *Animal Farm*.

All animals are equal, but some animals are more equal than others.

Animal Farm

1949	Published *Nineteen Eighty-Four* (the date being a reversal of the year he wrote it, 1948), his second political satire.

Who controls the past controls the future: who controls the present controls the past.

Nineteen Eighty-Four

Don't you see that the whole aim of Newspeak is to narrow the range of thought? In the end we shall make thoughtcrime literally impossible, because there will be no words in which to express it.

Ibid.

Freedom is the freedom to say that two plus two makes four. If that is granted, all else follows.

Ibid.

If you want a picture of the future, imagine a boot stamping on a human face — forever!

Ibid.

DEATH	1950 aged 46, from tuberculosis, from which he had suffered for many years, on Islay in the Inner Hebrides. Buried in All Saints' churchyard, Sutton Courtenay, Oxfordshire.
HOBBIES & INTERESTS	Knitting.

Sir John Betjeman

British Poet Laureate, described by The Times *as, 'By Appointment: Teddy Bear to the Nation'.*

BIRTH 1906, Highgate, London, son of a manufacturer of household goods.

MARITAL STATUS Married, 1934, Penelope Chetwode. One son, Paul, and one daughter, Candida.

> 'We invite people like that to tea, but we do not marry them.'
> Lady Chetwode, his future mother-in-law, to her daughter on being first introduced

EDUCATION Marlborough College and Magdalen College, Oxford (left without taking his degree).

> I've often thought that I would like to be the saddle on a bike.
> Allegedly sole poetic output at Oxford

Honary degrees from Oxford, Reading, Birmingham, Exeter, City University, Liverpool, Hull and Trinity College, Dublin.

 ## A Little Bit of Background

The BBC began television broadcasting in 1929. The Second World War took place 1939–45. National Service was abolished in 1960. Neil Armstrong walked on the moon in 1969.

CAREER

1929	Schoolmaster.
1930	Assistant Editor, the *Architectural Review*.
1930	First poem, *Death in Leamington*, appeared in the *London Mercury*.
1931	Wrote for the *Architectural Review*.

1931	Published *Mount Zion*, his first collection of verse.
1933	Film critic for the *Evening Standard*.
1933	Published *Ghastly Good Taste* on Architecture.

> Ghastly good taste, or a depressing story of the
> rise and fall of English architecture
>
> *Book title, 1933*

1937	Published *Continual few: a little book of bourgeois verse.*

> Come, friendly bombs, and fall on Slough!
> It isn't fit for humans now,
> There isn't grass to graze a cow.
>
> *Slough, 1937*

1939	Worked in the Films Division of the Ministry of Information.
1940	Published *Old Lights for New Chancels.*

> Think of what our Nation stands for,
> Books from Boots' and country lanes
> Free speech, free passes, class distinction,
> Democracy and proper drains.
>
> *In Westminster Abbey, 1940*

1941	UK Press Attaché, Dublin, and then in the Admiralty 'P' branch.
1945	Published *New Bats in Old Belfries.*

> Love-thirty, love-forty, oh! weakness of joy,
> The speed of a swallow, the grace of a boy,
> With carefullest carelessness, gaily you won,
> I am weak from your loveliness, Joan Hunter Dunn.
> Miss Joan Hunter Dunn, Miss Joan Hunter Dunn,
> How mad I am, sad I am, glad that you won.
>
> *A Subaltern's Love-Song, 1945*

1950–60	Book reviewing and broadcasting.
1954	Published *A few Late Chrysanthemums.*

> And is it true? And is it true,
> This most tremendous tale of all,
> Seen in a stained-glass window's hue,
> A Baby in an ox's stall?
> The Maker of the stars and sea
> Become a Child on earth for me?
>
> *Christmas,* 1954

1958	Published *Collected Poems*. (Expanded 1962.)
1960	Awarded Queen's Medal for Poetry and made CBE.
	Published *Summoned by Bells*, a Blank Verse Autobiography.

> The dread of beatings! Dread of being late!
> And, greatest dread of all, the dread of games!
>
> *Summoned by Bells,* 1960

1966	Published *High and Low*.
1969	Knighted.
1972	Published *A Nip in the Air*.
	Poet Laureate.
1982	Wrote and edited Shell Guides.
	Published *Uncollected Poems*.
DEATH	1984, aged 78. Buried St Enodoc Church, Trebetherick, Cornwall.
HOBBIES & INTERESTS	Saving buildings threatened with destruction.

Philip Larkin

Post-war British poet and librarian, who echoed the nostalgia of millions in his three collections of poetry.

BIRTH	1922, in Coventry.
MARITAL STATUS	Single.
EDUCATED	Henry VIII school, Coventry, St John's College, Oxford, where he was a contemporary, and friend, of the novelist Kingsley Amis. Honorary degrees from Belfast, Leicester, Warwick, St Andrews, Sussex and Oxford.

 ## A Little Bit of Background

Queen Elizabeth II was crowned in 1953. Rationing ended in 1954. The Beatles reached No. 1 in 1962. The UK joined the Common Market in 1973.

CAREER	
1943–6	Librarian, Wellington, Shropshire.
1944/5	Some early poems published in *Poetry from Oxford in Wartime* and *The North Ship*.
1946–50	Assistant Librarian, Leicester University.
1946	Published *Jill*, a novel.
1947	Published his second novel, *A Girl in Winter*.
1950–5	Sub-Librarian, Queen's University, Belfast.

> Nothing, like something, happens anywhere.
>
> '*I Remember, I Remember*', 1955

> Why should I let the toad work
> Squat on my life?
> Can't I use my wit as a pitchfork
> And drive the brute off?
>
> '*Toads*', 1955

1955–85	Librarian, Brynmor Jones Library, Hull University.
1956	Published a book of poetry, *The Less Deceived*.
1961–71	Jazz reviewer for the *Daily Telegraph*.
1964	Published a further book of poetry, *The Whitsun Weddings*.

> What are days for?
> Days are where we live.
>
> 'Days', 1964

1965	Won the Queen's Gold Medal for Poetry.
1970	Jazz reviews collected in *All What Jazz*.
1970–1	Visiting Fellow, All Souls, Oxford.
1973	Published *The Oxford Book of Twentieth-Century Verse*.
1974	Published a third book of poetry, *High Windows*.

> Sexual intercourse began
> In nineteen sixty-three
> (Which was rather late for me) –
> Between the end of the *Chatterley* ban
> And the Beatles' first LP.
>
> 'Annus Mirabilis', 1974
>
> They fuck you up, your mum and dad.
> They may not mean to, but they do.
> They fill you with the faults they had
> And add some extra, just for you.
>
> 'This Be The Verse', 1974

1975	CBE (Companion of the British Empire).
1977	Chairman of the Poetry Book Society.
	Chairman of the Booker Prize Judges.
1983	Book Reviews collected in *Required Writing*.
1984	Declined offer to become Poet Laureate.

> I am afraid the compulsion to write poems left me about seven years ago, since when I have written virtually nothing. Naturally this is a disappointment, but I would sooner write no poems than bad poems.
>
> Letter, 11 August 1984, *Selected Letters of Philip Larkin*, ed. Anthony Thwaite, 1992

1985	CH (Companion of Honour).
DEATH	1985 aged 63, of throat cancer in Hull. Buried at Holy Cross Church, Cottingham, Hull.
HOBBIES & INTERESTS	Jazz.

Margaret Thatcher

*Margaret Hilda Thatcher, later Baroness Thatcher of
Kesteven, British Conservative stateswoman dubbed the Iron
Lady by the Soviet* Red Star. *The longest-serving British
Prime Minister of the Twentieth Century.*

BIRTH	1925, as Margaret Roberts, in Grantham, Lincolnshire. Father a grocer and alderman.
MARITAL STATUS	Married, 1951, Denis Thatcher, d. 2003. One son and one daughter (twins, Carol and Mark).
EDUCATION	Kesteven and Grantham Girls' School, Somerville College, Oxford.

 ## A Little Bit of Background

Jim Callaghan's Labour Government was in power during the 1978–9 'Winter of Discontent', which was marked by exceptional levels of industrial unrest. Ronald Reagan was elected President of the United States in 1980. The Falklands War took place in 1982. 1984 saw the Miner's Strike, and 1989 the tearing down of the Berlin Wall.

CAREER	
1947–51	Research chemist.
1954	Called to the Bar, Lincoln's Inn.
1959–92	MP for Finchley, London.
1961–4	Joint Parliamentary Secretary, Ministry of Pensions and National Insurance.
1970	Privy Councillor and Honorary Fellow of Somerville College, Oxford.
1971–4	Secretary of State for Education and Science.
1975–9	Leader of the Opposition.

In politics if you want anything said, ask a man. If you want anything done, ask a woman.

In *People Magazine* (New York), 15 September 1975

'I stand before you tonight in my red chiffon evening gown, my face softly made up, my fair hair gently waved . . . the Iron Lady of the Western World! Me? A cold war warrior? Well, yes — if that is how they wish to interpret my defence of values and freedoms fundamental to our way of life.'

Speech, Finchley, 31 January 1976

The Iron Lady.

Name given to Thatcher by the Soviet defence ministry newspaper *Red Star*, which accused her of trying to revive the cold war, quoted in the *Sunday Times*, 25 January 1976

'Britain is no longer the politics of the pendulum, but of the ratchet.'

Speech, Institute of Public Relations, 1977

1979–90	Prime Minister and First Lord of the Treasury.

'Pennies don't fall from heaven. They have to be earned on earth.'

'Sayings of the Week', *Observer* 18 November 1979

No one would remember the Good Samaritan if he'd only had good intentions. He had money as well.

Television interview, 6 January 1980, reported in *The Times*, 12 January 1980

'To those waiting with bated breath for that favourite media catchphrase, the U-turn, I have only this to say. "You turn if you want; the lady's not for turning."'

Speech at the Conservative Party Conference, Brighton, 10 October 1980

1982	Falklands War.

'Just rejoice at that news and congratulate our armed forces and the Marines. Rejoice!'

> On the recapture of South Georgia, usually quoted as 'Rejoice, rejoice!',
> to newsmen outside 10 Downing Street, 25 April 1982

1983 | Fellow of the Royal Society (FRS).

'I was asked whether I was trying to restore Victorian values. I said straight out I was. And I am.'

> Speech to the British Jewish Community, 21 July 1983,
> referring to an interview with Brian Walden on 17 January 1983

'I am painted as the greatest dictator – which is ridiculous – you always take some consultations.'

> 1983

1984 | Survived a terrorist attack by the IRA, which planted a bomb at the Grand Hotel, Brighton, where Thatcher and her Cabinet were staying for the duration of the Party Conference.

'This was the day I was meant not to see.'

> The day after the Brighton Bomb

'Now it must be business as usual.'

> On the steps of Brighton Police Station a few hours after the bombing of the Grand Hotel,
> Brighton; often quoted as 'we shall carry on as usual', reported in *The Times*, 13 October 1984

'We can do business together.'

> Of the Soviet leader, Mikhail Gorbachev, *The Times*, 18 December 1984

'I don't mind how much my ministers talk as long as they do what I say.'

> 1987

There is no such thing as Society. There are individual men and women, and there are families.

In *Woman's Own*, 31 October 1987

1990	OM.

'No! No! No!'

Speech making clear her opposition to a single European currency, and more centralised controls from Brussels, House of Commons, 30 October 1990

'It's a funny old world.'

On withdrawing from the contest for leadership of the Conservative party, 22 November 1990

Home is where you come to when you have nothing better to do.

Vanity Fair magazine, May 1991

1992	Chancellor, University of Buckingham.
2003	Widowed.

'Being PM is a lonely job. In a sense, it ought to be — you cannot lead from a crowd. But with Denis there I was never alone. What a man. What a husband. What a friend.'

Paying tribute to her husband on his death, 2003

HOBBIES & INTERESTS	Chemistry.

Queen Elizabeth II

Elizabeth Alexandra Mary, Queen of the United Kingdom of Great Britain and Northern Ireland since 1952, head of the British Commonwealth and Supreme Governor of the Church of England.

BIRTH | 1926, to the then Duke and Duchess of York .

MARITAL | Married, 1947, Philip Mountbatten of Greece, a distant cousin. Three sons, Charles, Andrew and Edward, and one daughter, Anne.

EDUCATION | Educated privately.

> 'I should like to be a horse.'
>
> Ambition as a child

 ## A Little Bit of Background

Stalin died in 1952. The Korean War took place 1952–3. Ghana gained independence in 1957, and Nigeria in 1960. Capital punishment was abolished in 1965. Homosexual acts and abortion were made legal in Britain in 1967. The UK joined the Common Market in 1973. The Falklands War took place in 1982. The Berlin Wall was torn down in 1989. In 1991, Britain signed the Maastricht Treaty and embarked on the first Gulf War and Sir Tim Berners Lee invented the World Wide Web. 1999 saw Devolution for Wales and Scotland.

CAREER

1936 | Became heir to the throne on the accession of her father, George VI, following the abdication of her uncle, Edward VIII.

1945 | Joined the Auxiliary Transport Services, where she learnt car mechanics.

'I declare before you all that my whole life, whether it be long or short, shall be devoted to your service and the services of our great Imperial family to which we all belong.'

Broadcast speech, as Princess Elizabeth, to the Commonwealth, Cape Town, 21 April 1947

1947	Married Philip Mountbatten, who was created Duke of Edinburgh on the eve of the wedding, in Westminster Abbey.
1948	Birth of Prince Charles, the Prince of Wales.
1950	Birth of Princess Anne, the Princess Royal.
1952	Proclaimed Queen on the death of her father, George VI.
1953	Crowned.
1960	Birth of Prince Andrew, the Duke of York.
1964	Birth of Prince Edward, the Earl of Wessex.

'I think everybody really will concede that on this, of all days, I should begin my speech with the words, "My husband and I".'

Speech, Guildhall, London, on her 25th wedding anniversary, 1972

1977	Celebrated her Silver Jubilee.
1992	Her '*annus horribilis*'. The year in which two of her children's marriages failed and parts of Windsor Castle were severely damaged by fire.

'In the words of one of my more sympathetic correspondents, it has turned out to be an "*annus horribilis*".'

Speech, Guildhall, London, 24 November 1992

1997	The death of Diana, Princess of Wales.

'I sometimes sense the world is changing almost too fast for its inhabitants, at least for us older ones.'

On her tour of Pakistan, 8 October 1997

'Think what we would have missed if we had never . . . used a mobile phone or surfed the Net or, to be honest, listened to other people talking about surfing the Net.'

Reflecting on developments over the past 50 years, the *Daily Telegraph*, 21 November 1997

| **2002** | Celebrated her Golden Jubilee. |

'...those who perpetrate these brutal acts against innocent people should know that they will not change our way of life. Atrocities such as these simply reinforce our sense of community, our humanity, and our trust in the rule of Law. That is the clear message from us all.'

Speech at the Royal London Hospital after the terrorist blast in Central London, having defied the security services to visit the casualties, 8 July 2005

| **HOBBIES & INTERESTS** | Her subjects, the Commonwealth, the Church of England, horses and dogs. |

Gazetteer

Locations of burial sites.

ENGLAND

BERKSHIRE
BISHAM:
Bisham Abbey
  Warwick the Kingmaker   43
READING:
Reading Abbey:
  before the High Altar
  Henry I   20
WINDSOR:
Frogmore Mausoleum
  Queen Victoria   219
St George's Chapel
  Charles I   89
  George III   154
  Henry VIII   54

BUCKINGHAMSHIRE
BEACONSFIELD:
Beaconsfield Church
  Edmund Burke   151
HUGHENDEN:
Hughenden Manor
  Benjamin Disraeli   197

CORNWALL
TREBETHERICK:
St Enodoc's Churchyard
  Sir John Betjeman   258

CUMBRIA
GRASMERE:
St Oswald's Churchyard
  William Wordsworth   171

DURHAM
DURHAM CATHEDRAL:
Galilee Chapel
  The Venerable Bede   8

ESSEX
HIGH LAVER:
All Saints' Churchyard
  John Locke   103

HAMPSHIRE
WINCHESTER:
Hyde Abbey
  Alfred the Great   12
Winchester Cathedral
  Jane Austen   174

KENT
CANTERBURY:
Canterbury Cathedral
  St Dunstan   14
Roper Vault
  Sir Thomas More's head   47

LEICESTERSHIRE
MORETON SAY:
St Margaret's Churchyard
  Clive of India   142

LONDON

BARKING:
Friends Burial Ground
Elizabeth Fry   181

CITY:
Bunhill Fields Burial Ground, City
Road, EC1
John Bunyan   97
William Blake   156
George Fox (*though his grave
is no longer identifiable due
to bomb damage*)   95
Church of St Peter ad Vincula, EC3
Sir Thomas More   47
City Road Chapel, EC1
John Wesley   122
St Bride's Fleet Street, Bride Lane,
EC4
Samuel Richardson   120
St Giles's Church without
Cripplegate, London Wall
John Milton   92
St Paul's Cathedral
Lord Nelson   159
J.M.W. Turner   177
The Duke of Wellington   166
Sir Christopher Wren   106

GREENWICH:
St Alphege's, Greenwich High Road,
SE10
General Wolfe   147

HAMPSTEAD:
St John's, Church Row, NW3
John Constable   179

KENSAL GREEN:
Kensal Green Cemetery
Isambard Kingdom Brunel   202
Anthony Trollope   217

KENSINGTON:
Brompton Cemetery, Fulham Road,
SW10
Mrs Pankhurst   235

KEW:
St Anne's, Kew Green, Richmond
Thomas Gainsborough   145

KING'S CROSS:
King's Cross Station: beneath
Platform 8
Boadicea   2

WESTMINSTER:
St Margaret's, Parliament Square,
SW1
Sir Walter Ralegh   71
Westminster Abbey
Charles II   100
Edward I   26
Edward III   31
Elizabeth I   61
Henry V   38
James I   83
Mary Queen of Scots   69
Mary I   59
William of Orange   113
Florence Nightingale   222
Lord Palmerston   185
William Makepeace
Thackeray   209
William Wilberforce   164
Nave
Charles Darwin   204
Sir Isaac Newton   108
North Transept
William Gladstone   206
William Pitt the Elder   129
William Pitt the Younger   162
Poets' Corner

Geoffrey Chaucer 34
Charles Dickens 212
Dr Johnson 131
Rudyard Kipling 240
Edmund Spenser 74

NOTTINGHAMSHIRE
HUCKNALL TORKARD:
Byron Vault
Lord Byron 188

OXFORDSHIRE
BLADON:
St Martin's Churchyard
Sir Winston Churchill 245
BLENHEIM:
Blenheim Palace Chapel
Duke of Marlborough 110
SUTTON COURTENAY:
All Saints' Churchyard
George Orwell 255

WARWICKSHIRE
Stratford-upon-Avon:
Holy Trinity
William Shakespeare 78

WORCESTERSHIRE
LITTLE MALVERN:
St Wulfstan's Church
Edward Elgar 233

YORKSHIRE
HULL:
Holy Cross Church, Cottingham
Philip Larkin 261

SCOTLAND

DUNFERMLINE
MELROSE ABBEY
Robert the Bruce 29

EDINBURGH
CANONGATE KIRKYARD
Adam Smith 139

WALES

LLANYSTUMDWY:
On the bank of the River Dwyfor
David Lloyd George 237

NORTHERN IRELAND

BELFAST
St Anne's Cathedral
Edmund Carson 230

COUNTY DOWN
DOWNPATRICK:
At the foot of Cathedral Hill
St Patrick 4

REPUBLIC OF IRELAND

DUBLIN
St Patrick's Cathedral
Jonathan Swift 115

Index

Act of Settlement 114, 138
Adela of Louvain 20, 21
Aethelbert, King 11
Afghanistan 264
Agincourt, battle of 39
Alban, Saint 11
Albert, Prince 219, 220
Alexander the Great 42
Alfred, King 10, 12–13,
  271
America 96, 122–3,
  149–50, 152, 154, 169,
  210–11, 213, 218,
  234–5, 240, 251
American Civil War 185,
  187, 212, 222, 223
American Independence
  122, 129, 149, 151, 155,
  162
Amundsen, Roald 243
Andrew, Prince 268, 269
Angles 10, 12–13
Anglicans 52, 74, 122
Anglo-Irish War 230, 237
Anne, Queen 108–12, 118,
  131
Anne, Princess 268, 269
Anne of Cleves 54, 56
Anne of Denmark 83, 84, 89
Antarctica 149–50, 243,
  244
Armstrong, Neil 258
Arthur, King 42
Arthur, Prince of Wales 54
Astor, Nancy 246
Athelstan, King 14
Aubrey, John 62
Augustine, Saint 6–7
Austen, Jane 171, 174–6,
  271
Australia 149, 181, 218,
  254
Austria 129, 186

Babington Plot 62–3, 70
Baker, Hermione 225
Balestier, Caroline 240
Balliol, John 29

Bank of England 103
Barbazan, Sire de 40
Barlow, W. 84
Barnardo, Thomas 181
Barnet, battle of 44
Barry, Charles 197, 219
Basire, James 156
Batts, Elizabeth 149
Bavarians 111
Beagle (ship) 204
Beatles 261, 262
Beauchamp, Anne de 43
Beaufort, Henry 38
Beaumont, Sir George 173
Becket, Thomas 23
Bede 8–9, 271
Belgium 41, 112, 186
Bengal, Nawab of 143
Bennet, Gervase 96
Berlin Wall 264, 268
Bertha, Queen 6
Berwick, Treaty of 90
Betjeman, Sir John 258–60,
  271
Bible 41, 57, 83, 84, 92, 94
Bicknell, Maria 179, 180
Bill of Rights 1689 113
Biscop, Benedict 8
Blake, William 156–8, 171,
  272
Blenheim, battle of 111
Boadicea vii, 2–3, 272
Boer Wars 221, 225–6,
  228, 237, 240, 245
Boleyn, Anne 46–7, 52,
  54–5, 61
Bolingbroke, Henry 36
Book of Common Prayer 65–6,
  88, 100
Boston Tea Party 122
Boswell, James 132–6
Bosworth, battle of 43
Bothwell, Earl of 69, 70
Boucher, Catherine 156
Bourchier, Elizabeth 85
Boyle, Elizabeth 74, 75
Boyne, battle of the 106,
  114, 116

Brawne, Fanny 195
Breakespear, Nicolas 22
Bretigny, Treaty of 33
Bridgewater Canal 122,
  139, 202
British Army 220, 226
British Broadcasting
  Corporation (BBC) 258
British fleet 13, 31, 118,
  137, 149–50, 159, 161,
  243, 246
Bronté, Duke of 160
Brontë sisters 174
Brooke, Rupert 251–2
Bruce, Kathleen 243
Brunel, Isambard Kingdom
  202–3, 272
Buccleuch, Duke of 139
Buchanan, George 83
Bulwer-Lytton, Edward 200
Bunyan, John 97–9, 272
Burke, Edmund 151–3, 271
Burma 253, 254, 255
Burne-Jones, Edward 240
Burney, Fanny 155
Burr, Margaret 145
Bute, Lord 134
Byron, Augusta 188, 189
Byron, Lord 188–91, 195,
  273

Caesar, Julius 42
Callaghan, Jim 264
Calvert, Raisley 171
Calvin, John 55
Canada 129, 147–8, 162,
  219, 251
Canute, King 14
Cape St Vincent, battle of
  160
Carey, Henry 78
Caroline, Queen 119
Carson, Edward 230–2,
  273
Catherine of Aragon 45–7,
  52, 54–5, 59, 101
Catherine of Braganza 100,
  142

Catherine of France 38, 40
Catherine the Great 119
Catholicism 52–3, 56, 59,
   61, 67, 69–70, 76, 90,
   95, 97, 102, 114, 138,
   151, 169, 192
Catus Decianus 2
Cavaliers 85
Caxton, William 41–2
Cecil, Robert 64
Cervantes 78
Chaplin, Charlie 243
Charlemagne 11, 42
Charles, Prince 268, 269
Charles I, King 83–4, 86,
   89–93, 95, 97, 100,
   103, 108, 113, 271
Charles II, King 85, 89, 92,
   94–5, 97, 100–3, 106,
   108, 272
Charles V, King of Spain 52
Charlie, Bonnie Prince
   129, 137–8, 147
Charlotte Sophia of
   Mecklenburg-Strelitz
   154
Chastelard 70
Chaucer, Geoffrey 34–5,
   42, 273
Chaumpaigne, Cecilia 35
Chesterfield, Lord 132
Chetwode, Penelope 258
China 185, 206
Christianity 4–8, 42
Church of England 52, 53,
   55
Churchill, Lord Randolf
   245
Churchill, Sir Winston
   245–50, 273
Clairmont, Claire 188
Clarke, John 195
Claudius 2
Cleveland, Duchess of 110
Clive, Edward 142
Clive of India (Robert
   Clive) 142–4, 271
Coghill, Faith 106
Coleridge, Samuel Taylor
   156, 171
Colt, Jane 47
Common Market 261, 268
Conservative Party 192
Constable, John 179–80,
   272

Conway, Treaty of 24
Cook, Captain James
   149–50
Cooper, Anthony Ashley
   103
Corn Laws 192, 194, 198,
   219
Cowper, Lady 185
Cradock, Charlotte 126,
   127
Cranmer, Thomas 52–3, 55
Crimean War 181, 185,
   197, 206, 212, 219–20,
   222
Cromwell, Oliver 85,
   85–8, 92
Cromwell, Thomas 56
Crusaders 20, 22, 27
Cuba 245
Curia Regis 20, 22
Curthose, Robert 18–21
Cyprus 200, 225

Danby, Sarah 177
Danes 12–14, 167
Daniel, Mary 126
Darnley, Earl of 69, 70, 83
Darwin, Charles 204–5,
   272
David 42
David II, King of Scotland
   29
Davys, Revd George 219
De Beers 228–9
de Grey, Reginald 36
de Montfort, Eleanor 24
de Montfort, Simon 24, 26
de Valera, Eamon 239
de Vere, Edward 62
Delaborde, Marshal 167
D'Ewes, Sir Simonds 63
Diana, Princess of Wales
   269
Dickens, Charles 209,
   212–16, 273
Discovery (ship) 243
Disraeli, Benjamin
   197–201, 271
D'Israeli, Isaac 197
Domesday Book 19
Dover, Treaty of 102
Drake, Sir Francis 67–8
Drummond, William 70
Dudley 54
Dunstan, Saint 14–15, 271

Dutch 84, 102, 113, 143

Ealdgyth 16
Ealhswith, Queen 12
East India Company 142–3,
   206, 209
Easter Rising 230
Echlin, Lady 121
Edgar, King 14–15
Edgehill, battle of 90
Edict of Nantes 61
Edinburgh, Prince Philip,
   Duke of 268, 269
Edith, Queen 16
Edmund, King 14
Edmund of Langley 31
Edred, King 14
Edward I, King 15, 24,
   26–8, 29–30, 272
Edward II, King 26, 30, 31
Edward III, King 31–4, 272
Edward IV, King 41, 44
Edward VI, King 50, 52,
   54, 59, 65–6
Edward VII, King 220
Edward VIII, King 245,
   247, 268
Edward the Black Prince
   31, 33
Edward the Confessor, St
   16, 19
Edward, Duke of Kent 219
Edward, Prince 268, 269
Edwy, King 14
Egypt 186, 217, 222, 225–6
Einstein, Albert 243
Eleanor of Aquitaine 22, 23
Eleanor of Castile 26
Eleanor of Provence 26
Elgar, Sir Edward 233–4,
   273
Elizabeth I, Queen vii, 54,
   61–5, 67–8, 70–2,
   74–5, 78, 83, 272
Elizabeth II, Queen 245,
   261, 268–70
Elizabeth de Burgh 29
Elizabeth of France 66
Empson 54
Endeavour (ship) 149
engineering 183–4, 202–3
English Civil War 85, 103
Erasmus 47, 57
Eritrea 253
Essex, Earl of 63–4, 72

Ethandun 12
Ethelbert, King 6
Ethelred I, King 12
Eugene, Prince 111
Evolution 204–5

Fairfax, Lord General 93,
    100
Falklands War 264, 265–6,
    268
Fell, Margaret 95
Fielding, Edmund 126
Fielding, Henry 120,
    126–8, 131
First World War 225, 230,
    233, 236–8, 240, 242,
    245–6, 251
Fisher, John 55, 179, 180
Floyd, Julia 192
Foster, Sarah 230, 231
Fox, George 95–6, 181,
    272
France 32–4, 37, 39–40,
    43–4, 54, 61, 69–70,
    83, 89, 104, 111–12,
    122, 129, 137–8, 142–3,
    147, 151, 154, 159, 160,
    162–3, 168, 171, 174,
    177, 179, 185–6, 202,
    209, 226, 246, 248
Francis I, King 46, 48, 54
Francis II, King 69
Franco-Prussian War 222,
    223
Frederick Louis, Prince
    154
French Revolution 151,
    154, 159, 171
Freud, Sigmund 243
Frewen, Ruby 230
Fry, Elizabeth 181–2, 222,
    272
Fry, Joseph 181
Fuller, Thomas 71

Gainsborough, Thomas
    145–6, 272
Galileo 83
Garrick, David 131
Gatling, Dr 225
Gaveston, Piers 31
General Strike 1926 245
George I, King 108, 112,
    118
George II, King 118

George III, King 131, 134,
    154–6, 219, 271
George IV, King 154, 155
George VI, King 268, 269
Germany 41, 112, 171,
    220, 251
Ghana 268
Gilbert, Sir Humphrey 71
Gladstone, William 187,
    206–8, 220–1, 272
Glendower, Owen 36–7
Glorious Revolution 1688
    97, 103
Glynne, Catherine 206
Godfrey of Bouillon 42
Godwin, Earl 16
Gorbachev, Mikhail 266
Gordon Riots 155
Granville, Lady Hester 129
Great Exhibition 1851 166,
    202, 206, 209–10, 219
Great Fire Of London 97,
    100–1, 106–7
Great Reform Bill 166
Greece 185, 186, 188, 189,
    191
Gregory I, Pope 6, 12–13
Grey, Lady Jane 53, 59
Gulf War 268
Gunpowder Plot 78, 84
Guthrum 12
Gwyn, Nell 102
Gytha of Wessex 16

Hadrian I, Pope 10
Hamilton, Lady 159, 160,
    161
Hamilton, William Gerard
    151
Hamner, Margaret 36
Handel, George Frideric
    120
Harold Hardrada 17
Harold II, King 16–19
Harvey, William 89
Hastings, battle of 16, 17,
    18
Hastings, Warren 152
Hathaway, Anne 78
Hawkins, John 67
Hector of Troy 42
Hedley, William 183
Henderson, Frances 183
Henrietta Maria, Princess
    89

Henry I, King 18, 20–2,
    271
Henry II, King 22–3
Henry III, King 24, 26
Henry IV, King of England
    36, 38
Henry IV, King of France
    83
Henry V, King 37, 38–41,
    272
Henry VI, King 38, 41, 43,
    44
Henry VII, King 45, 54, 69
Henry VIII, King 45, 47–8,
    50, 52, 54–9, 61, 65,
    220, 271
Henry, Prince of Wales 83,
    89
Henry the Navigator 38
Hereward the Wake 18
Hertford, Earl of 65, 66
Heseltine, Rose 217
Hindley, Elizabeth 183
Hitler, Adolf 239
Hogarth, Catherine 212
Hogarth, William 120, 145
Holland 89, 96, 102, 104,
    110–11, 114, 126, 147
Hong Kong 185
Hooke, Robert 109
Horsley, Mary 202
Howard, Catherine 54, 56
Hozier, Clementine 245,
    246
Hume, David 64, 73
Hundred Years War 32, 34,
    43
Hutchinson, Mary 171
Huxley, Aldous 205

Iceni tribe 2–3
India 129, 142–3, 147,
    162, 166–7, 186, 206,
    221, 226, 240, 245, 253
Indian Mutiny 142, 185,
    197, 219, 220
Iraq 253
Ireland 4–5, 16, 23, 71,
    74–5, 96, 111, 114,
    115, 124, 148, 151, 166,
    167, 173, 206, 207, 209,
    225, 230–2
Irish Civil War 230
Irish Potato Famine 192,
    194

Index

Irish Republican Army
(IRA) 266
Isabella of France 31, 32
Isabella of Mar 29
Italy 177, 190–1, 196, 198,
214, 220, 222

Jackson, William 145
Jacobite Rebellions 129,
138, 147
Jaffa, Emir of 27
James I, King of England
69–72, 78, 83–4, 89,
272
James II, King of England
89, 95, 97, 102–3, 106,
108, 110–11, 113–14,
118, 137–8
James V, King of Scotland
56, 69
Japan 253
Jennings, Sarah 110, 112
Jerome, Jennie 245
Jesus Christ 57, 62, 123
Jews 27, 42, 197
John, King 22
John of Gaunt 31, 34, 35
Johnson, Esther 115, 117
Johnson, Samuel 120–1,
126–7, 131–6, 174, 273
Jonson, Ben 70, 80, 81, 82
Joseph, King 167
Joshua, Duke 42
Judas Macabeus 42
Junot, Marshal 167

Keats, John 74, 195–6
Keats, Tom 196
Kipling, Rudyard 240–2,
273
Kitchener, Lord 225–7
Knox, John 65, 70
Korean War 268

Labour Party 235
Laing, Samuel 17
Lancastrians 41, 43, 44
Lanfranc, Archbishop 18
Lansdowne, Lord 221
Larkin, Philip 261–3, 273
Latimer, Hugh 50–1
Laud, Archbishop 90
Law, Bonar 246
Leake, Elizabeth 120
Lee, Tim Berners 268

Lehzen, Fraulein Louise
219
Leicester, Earl of 74, 78
Lepanto, battle of 61
Lewes, battle of 26
Lewis, Mary Anne 197, 198
Lindesfarne Gospels 9
Linnell, John 158
Lionel of Antwerp 31
Llewellyn ab Gruffydd 16,
17, 24–5, 27, 36
Lloyd, Edward 103
Lloyd George, David
237–9, 273
Lobengula, King 229
Locke, John 103–5, 271
Louis XIV, King 89, 101,
102, 110–11
Low Countries 41, 62
Luxembourg 114

MacAlpin, Kenneth 29
Macdonald, Flora 137
Machiavelli, Niccolò 55
Malcolm III, King 19–21
Malmesbury, William of 21
Malory, Thomas 41, 42
Malta 189
Mansfield, Lord 164
Margaret (of Scotland), St
20, 21
Margaret of Anjou 43, 44
Marguerite of France 26
Marie Antoinette 153
Markland, Jeremiah 136
Marlborough, Duke of
110–12, 273
Marlowe, Christopher
76–7
Marmont, Marshal 167
Martin Luther 45, 50, 55,
57
Martin of Tours 4
Marx, Karl 205
Mary I, Tudor 50–3, 54,
59–60, 61, 69, 272
Mary II, Queen 89, 97,
103, 108, 110, 113–14,
118, 138
Mary of Guise 70
Mary, Queen of Scots 62,
63, 69–70, 74, 83, 272
Masham, Lady 105
Maskelyne, Margaret 142
Massena, Marshal 167

Matilda (of Henry I) 20–2
Matilda (of Malcolm III)
20–1
Matilda of Flanders 18
Melville, Sir James 62
Methodists 120, 122–4
Miliuc 4
Mill, John Stewart 103
Millbanke, Anne Isabella
188, 189
Milton, John 92–4, 272
Minden, battle of 147
Miner's Strike 264
Minshull, Elizabeth 92, 94
Monmouth, Duke of 97,
100, 101, 103, 111
Moore, Thomas 189
Moravians 122, 123, 124
More, Sir Thomas 47–9,
55, 58, 271, 272
Mortimer, Sir Edmund 36
Mortimer, Roger 31, 32

Nanfan, Sir Richard 45
Napoleon 166, 168
Napoleonic Wars 162, 163,
166, 168
Naseby, battle of 90
Natural Selection 204
Neale, Sir John 63
Nelson, Lord Horatio vii,
159–61, 175, 272
Nero 2
Netherlands, The 77, 166
New Model Army 85, 86
New Zealand 149, 218–19,
251
Newman, Mary 67
Newton, Sir Isaac vii, 103,
106, 108–9, 272
Nicholas I, Tsar 169
Nietzche, Friedrich 205
Nightingale, Florence 181,
222–4, 272
Nile, battle of the 160
Nimegnen, Treaty of 113
Nisbet, Francis 159, 160
Nobel, Alfred 225
Norfolk, Duke of 62, 70
Normans 16–19, 20, 21,
23, 24
Northern Ireland 4–5, 232
Nottingham, Countess of
64
Nottingham, Earl of 76

Nugent, Jane 151
Nun of Kent, The 55

Oates, Captain 244
O'Connell, Daniel 192
Offa 10–11
Opium Wars 185, 206
Orwell, George 255–7, 273
O'Shaugnessey, Eileen 255
Owen, Margaret 237
Oxford, Edward 220

Pakenham, Katherine 166
Palestine 22
Palmerston, Lord 185–7,
    207, 217, 272
Pankhurst, Christabel 235
Pankhurst, Mrs (Emmeline
    Goulden) 235–6, 272
Pankhurst, R.M. 235
Parker, Colonel 111
Parliament 20, 22, 27, 31,
    39, 84–5, 87–90,
    112–13, 152–3, 164,
    169, 192, 212
Parr, Catherine 54, 56
Patrick, Saint 4–6, 273
Paulinus, Suetonius 2, 3
Peasants' Revolt 34
Peel, Sir Robert 192–4
Penny Post 171, 217
People's Budget 237
Percy, Henry (Hotspur) 37
Peterloo Massacre 192
Philip II of Spain 83
Philip IV of France 31
Philip of Burgundy 43
Philip the Magnanimous 58
Philip of Spain 59, 60, 70
Philippa of Hainault 31, 32
Picts 4, 5
Pilgrim Fathers 83
Pitt, William (Pitt the
    Elder) 126, 129–30,
    162, 272
Pitt, William (Pitt the
    Younger) 129, 162–3,
    272
plague 31–4, 97, 100, 108
Plantagenets 22
Poitiers, battle of 32
police 192
Porter, 'Tetty' 131
Portugal 38, 126, 128, 142,
    167, 186, 189

Powell, Mary 92, 93
Prasutagus 2
printing press 41–2
Proclamation Society 164
Protestantism 45, 47, 50–1,
    55–61, 65, 67, 69–70,
    76, 83, 89, 95, 122, 151

Quakers (Society of
    Friends) 95–6, 98, 181
Queensberry, Lord 230

railways 183–4, 202, 212
Ralegh, Sir Walter 61,
    71–3, 84, 272
Reagan, Ronald 264
Red Cross 222
Reform Act 1832 185, 192,
    197, 212
Reformation 55
Renaissance 47
Resolution (ship) 149
Reynolds, Sir Joshua 145,
    156, 177
Rhodes, Cecil 228–9
Rhodesia 229
Riccio 70
Richard I, King 22
Richard II, King 31, 35, 36,
    38
Richard, Duke of York 43,
    44
Richard, Earl of Salisbury
    43
Richardson, Samuel 120–1,
    126, 127, 131, 133, 174,
    272
Richelieu, Cardinal 89
Ridley, Latimer 65
Ridley, Nicholas 51
Robert the Bruce 28,
    29–30, 273
Robert, Duke of Kintyre
    and Lorne 83
Robert, Duke of
    Normandy 18
Roberts, Alice 233, 234
Robertson, Aileen 253
Robin of Redesdale 44
Rochester, Earl of 101
Rockingham, Marquis of
    151
Rollo the Viking 19
Romans 2, 5–6, 9, 11, 24,
    29

Rome 12, 17, 54, 55, 65,
    84, 137, 138, 190, 196
Roosevelt, Franklin D. 249
Roper, William 48
Roses, War of the 41, 43
Roundheads 85
Royal Academy 145, 146,
    156, 157, 177, 179
Royal Mint 108, 109
Royal Society 100, 103,
    106–9, 266
Ruskin, John 178
Russia 186
Russian Revolution 255

St Albans, battles of 43–4
Saladin 22
Salisbury, Lord 221
Savory, Thomas 183
Saxons 6, 10, 12–13, 14,
    16, 20
Schoberg, Duke of 116
Scotland/Scots 4–5, 19,
    22, 27–30, 32, 36, 38,
    54, 56, 69, 83, 86–7,
    90–1, 96, 100, 110,
    115, 124, 134, 137–9,
    147, 152, 172–3, 268
Scott, Captain 243–4
Scott, Sir Peter 243
Second World War 237,
    245, 253, 258
Seven Years' War 122, 129,
    147, 162
Seymour, Edward 65
Seymour, Jane 50, 54, 55,
    65
Shakespeare, William 76,
    78–82, 92, 134, 155,
    273
Shawe, Isabella 209
Shelley, Mary 174
Shelley, Percy Bysshe 74,
    195
Shorter, Catherine 118
Sidney, Sir Philip 74
slavery 83, 152, 164–5, 213
Slim, Field Marshal 253–4
Smith, Adam 131, 139–41,
    273
Smollett, Tobias 56, 127
Somers, Lord 63
Soult, Marshal 167, 168
South Africa 218, 228–9,
    241, 245

South Sea Company 115, 118, 119, 139
Spain/Spanish 32, 43, 67–8, 72–3, 83, 88, 160, 167, 169, 174, 186, 221, 245
Spanish Armada 61, 63, 68, 74, 76
Spanish Civil War 255, 256
Spanish Succession, War of the 110, 115
Spencer, Herbert 205
Spenser, Edmund 71, 74–5, 273
Spenser, Peregrine 74
Spooner, Barbara Ann 164
Spring, William 86
Stalin, Josef 255, 268
Stebbing, W. 73
Stephen, King 20
Stephenson, George 183–4
Stephenson, Robert 183, 184
Stevenson, Frances 237
Stigand, Archbishop 18
Stolberg, Louisa von 137, 138
Storey, Anne 108
Strange, Lord 78
Stratford, Edward 145
Sudan 225, 226, 228, 245
suffrage 235–6
Surrey, Earl of 56
Sweden 102
Sweyn of Denmark 18
Swift, Jonathan 115–17, 126, 273
Switzerland 186, 214, 220, 222
Syria 253

Temple, Sir William 115
Tenerife 160
Thackeray, William Makepeace 209–11, 217, 272
Thatcher, Denis 264, 267
Thatcher, Margaret 264–7
Thirty Years' War 83
Thomas of Woodstock 31

Throgmorton, Elizabeth 71–2
Tostig 17
Trafalgar, battle of 160–1, 174
Trevithick, Richard 202
Trollope, Anthony 212, 217, 272
Troyes, Treaty of 40
Turkey/Turks 55, 61, 185–6, 188, 189
Turner, J.M.W. 177–8, 272
Tyndale, William 48, 50, 57–8

Ulf 16

Vallon, Annette 171
Vazeille, Mary 122, 124
Versailles, Treaty of 154
Victor, Marshal 167
Victoria, Queen 197, 200, 201, 206, 219–21, 222, 229, 233, 271
Victoria of Saxe-Coburg 219
Victory (ship) 161
Vikings 9, 10, 12–13, 14, 17, 19

Wade, Marshall 147
Wales 2, 10–11, 16–17, 21, 24–5, 36–7, 55, 86, 135, 268
Walkinshaw, Clementina 137, 138
Wallace, William 28, 29
Walpole, Horace 118
Walpole, Sir Robert 118–19, 129
Walsingham, Sir Francis 68
Walter, Lucy 101
Warwick the Kingmaker vii, 41, 43–4, 271
Washington, George 151
Waterloo, battle of 166, 168, 174, 188, 195, 209
Watt, James 122, 183
Wedgwood, Emma 204
Wedgwood, Josiah 204

Wellington, Duke of (Arthur Wellesley) vii, 166–70, 174, 188, 193, 195, 209, 272
Wentworth, Lord 90
Wesley, Charles 122
Wesley, John 114, 120, 122–5, 272
West Indies 96, 159, 217
Wilberforce, William 152, 164–5, 272
Wilde, Martha 120
Wilde, Oscar 230
Wilkes, John 131
William I (the Conqueror) 16, 17, 18–19, 20, 103
William II (William Rufus) 18, 20–1
William II of Orange 113
William III (William of Orange) 95, 97, 104, 106, 108, 110, 111, 113–14, 116, 118, 138, 272
William IV, King 154
William the Atheling 20, 21
Wolfe, Edward 147
Wolfe, James 147–8, 272
Wolsey, Cardinal 45–6, 48, 50, 54–6, 58
Woodcock, Catherine 92, 94
Woodville, Elizabeth 44
Wordsworth, Dorothy 171
Wordsworth, William 156, 171–3, 195, 196, 271
World Wide Web (www) 268
Wren, Sir Christopher 106–7, 272
Wright Brothers 243
Wulcy, Robert 45
Wulfstan 14
Wycliffe, John 34, 38

Yorkists 41, 43–4, 56

Zimbabwe 229
Zulu War 228
Zwingli, Huldreich 58